The Epcot Explorer's Encyclopedia

R. A. Pedersen

EPCOT (n) – THAT PLACE WITH THE BIG SILVER BALL.

Contrary to popular belief, there's more to Epcot than just a very large silver ball. Certainly one could take Disney's own words on their website about the park at face value and just regard it as the place with a large golf-ball looking structure. This book is not for anyone of that mindset.

No, Epcot is so much more. As a theme park built at the apex of the art form with nearly three decades of growth behind it since the park's inception, Epcot stands as a fascinating and yet often entirely misunderstood monument to the human kind. This book is for the curious minds in the world who think there might be something more.

Will it be informative and entertaining? We hope so. As EPCOT Center proved when it opened, that can be a tricky balance to strike. With that in mind, let us begin at the beginning, for sing-song show tunes have suggested that's a very good place to start...

CONTENTS

ACKNOWLEDGMENTS

This book would not be possible without the assistance of numerous individuals, publications, and resources. We would like to acknowledge:

The Orlando Sentinel, The Chicago Sun Times, The Mesa Verde Times, Progress City USA, The EPCOT Discovery Center, Widen Your World, LOST Epcot, The Ocala Star-Banner, Intercot, The Palm Beach Post, Imaginerding, The Montreal Gazette, Horizons 1, The Pittsburg Press, Walt Dated World, The Milwaukee Journal, The Unofficial Guide, The Boca Raton News, The Telegraph, The Palm Beach Daily News, The Thinkwell Group, The Lakeland Ledger, Martins Vids, The Gainesville Sun, Eyes and Ears, The New York Times, Disney Echo, CBC News, The Daytona Beach Morning, Slate, AllEars, The Passporter, This Day in Disney History, D23, Playmotion, Central Florida Lifestyle, Mouseplanet, Imagineering Disney, The Internet Wayback Machine, The Universe of Energy Companion Site, Discussion Kingdom, The Themed Entertainment Association, The International Association of Amusement Parks and Attractions, and the Walt Disney Company.

Thank you.

1. WHAT'S IN A NAME?

A S ANYONE remotely familiar with the park can attest, there was a 99% probability this book would begin with the following sentence:

"EPCOT Center opened on October 1, 1982, at the Walt Disney World Resort..."

While true, this statement is troublesome. *Epcot* as it is branded today originally opened – formally in October of 1982 no less – as *EPCOT Center*. EPCOT was an acronym standing for Experimental Prototype Community of Tomorrow and the theme park itself was meant to be the center of this community, hence the name EPCOT Center. What was it the center of exactly...?

Walt Disney World!

All of the Walt Disney World resort is technically EPCOT. Now it's entirely understandable that if you're not as painfully familiar with Walt Disney World as the author of this book and certain internet personas that the previous statement might boggle the mind a bit. For the theme park's grand opening broadcast the Disney company took this into consideration and had the program's host, Danny Kaye, sing an entire song about what exactly an *EPCOT* is. We'll wait while you Google the song "Hooray for the 21st Century" and watch the video on YouTube.

Continuing on...

Walt Disney World, contrary to some plebeian beliefs, is not a single theme park. It's not even akin to its older sister the Disneyland Resort – which is a compartmentalized two-park complex in southern California surrounded on all sides by a sprawling urban landscape. At the Walt Disney World resort there are four theme parks (including Epcot), two water parks, an entertainment district, the remnants of a small airport, large swaths of nature preserve, and numerous resort hotels to fit all tastes and budgets.

Walt Disney World was intentionally built in the middle of relatively nowhere in central Florida. This way Disney was able to purchase lots of land really cheap – a really big piece of land. It's roughly twice the size of Manhattan or equivalent to San Francisco proper. The theme parks and the resorts are dotted around this chunk of land leaving wide swaths of greenery. The Epcot theme park is roughly in the middle of the abstract blob – one could even argue it's in the actual center.

Why so much land? And why refer to it as EPCOT?

Once upon a time, Walt Disney built the first real theme park in southern California and called it Disneyland and it was good. At first no one thought it would work, but it turns out it worked ridiculously well. So well in fact that all around the park other businesses started popping up hoping to feed off the success of Disneyland. The bigger those businesses got and the harder they tried to get their piece of the pie, the uglier and uglier it got around the Disneyland complex. The area came to define the term tourist trap.

We'll go out on a limb and call it *crap* and say that Disneyland was, within a few years, surrounded by crap that started to stink. Walt did not approve. The order was sent out to scout locations for a Disneyland 2.0 that could be constructed with a big buffer from the rest of the world. Just outside of Orlando, Florida, the location was settled on and a bunch of little companies working on behalf of Walt Disney started buying up the land. Now the plan wasn't to let all that extra land go to waste – not at all. Walt had decided on some really spectacular urban-planning with tiered living, green zones, and sci-fi style transportation systems to create a whole little futuristic community. The Experimental Prototype Community of Tomorrow to be exact. Disney had a place big enough to hold every dream there was to dream – and then some.

There needed to be rules for this little utopia though, and so the EPCOT building code was drawn up. Essentially any and all things were subject to approval of the company. The Reedy Creek Improvement District was formed as a governing body by some spectacular political aerobatics to oversee the whole of the EPCOT, establish the needed municipalities, and try and keep the crap out. No detail was overlooked in planning for the perfect community tasked with providing a living laboratory for innovative technologies and bringing various world cultures together as an international community.

However, somewhere in there Walt Disney passed away.

On December 15, 1966, to be precise. The Experimental Prototype Community of Tomorrow as planned wasn't anywhere near finished when it happened – in fact pretty much nothing was done. One man's dream was now the responsibility of hundreds who now lacked a guiding or driving force. The risk-adverse seized power and the financially palatable tried-and-true aspects of the project were allowed to go forward. Construction would begin the next year. The Disneyland 2.0 project opened as the Magic Kingdom on October 1, 1971, along with two resort hotels and a monorail line connecting them all. The whole place was named Walt Disney World in honor of the man. The people left behind sat around thinking about what to do now with the rest of the land.

Should they continue with the community, the city center, and the utopian idealism? Just opening the company's second theme park outside Orlando instead of any aspects of the planned community had already outwardly looked like a compromise of ideals. An era had ended and reality was setting in. The living laboratory idea, tasked with discovering solutions for the ills of the modern world, struggled on in a series of conferences around the country bearing the EPCOT name. Small satellite communities of thinkers were proposed to focus on different themes. The international culture complex was evolving separately of the futuristic theme center and both lingered listlessly as they underwent design revision after design revision. Dreams, it appeared, had limits and a tinge of cynicism began to creep in.

Just what would Disney do with all that land in Florida? The Magic Kingdom theme park and original resorts of Walt Disney World were doing remarkably well by the mid-1970s. Well enough to warrant expansion – well enough perhaps to warrant the building of a second theme park in Florida using all of that sprawling land. What about all the spectacular promises that had been made in regards to this patch of land?

Master Plan 5 was announced in the 1977 Walt Disney Productions Annual Report. The plan detailed the basic premise of the EPCOT Center theme park much as it would appear on opening day. Per the report:

> As conceived here, EPCOT will be a "Showcase for prototype concepts," demonstrating practical applications of new ideas and systems from creative centers everywhere. It will provide an "on-going forum of the future," where the best thinking of industry, government and academia is exchanged to communicate practical solutions to the needs of the world community. It will be a "communicator to the world," utilizing the growing spectrum of information transfer to bring new knowledge to the public. Finally, EPCOT will be a permanent "international people-to-people exchange," advancing the cause of world understanding.
>
> In addition, we are convinced that EPCOT will provide a much needed symbol of hope and

optimism that our major challenges can, and will be met. It will provide outstanding family entertainment from which people may draw enlightenment, as well as enjoyment. And it will, of course, represent a major new extension of our business activities around the world.

The project continued to evolve and changes to the park were still made, but the fundamental ideas were finally agreed upon. Hope and idealism reigned supreme. Soon shovels were working the earth to make EPCOT Center a reality. The dawn of the 21st century was about to begin.

2. LAY OF THE LAND

AFTER ALL OF THAT optimistic exuberance now might be a good time to simmer down and gather one's bearings in relation to the park itself. While it has been established that Epcot is a big deal, it's also pretty darn big. There is a lot of ground to cover and a basic understanding of the lay of the land (hence the title of this section) will prove insurmountably beneficial in the coming chapters. Not to mention, where else are we going to talk in painstaking detail about the parking lot?

As previously mentioned Epcot as we know it today started its life as EPCOT Center in late 1982. It has since evolved, changed names a few times, and even rebuilt entire areas of the park from the ground up. The park moved away from the *center of the perfect planned community* ideology in 1994 and was renamed *Epcot '94*. That idea lasted all of two years as the park was named *Epcot '95* for all of a month or two in 1995 and then finally just *Epcot* by 1996. The park retains the simpler Epcot name to this day. Despite Disney's best efforts to move away from the *EPCOT Center* moniker approximately 10% of internet searches for Epcot are for the term "EPCOT Center."

The 300 acre park-proper has always had two major sections, Future World and the World Showcase. Future World is geographically divided into three primary areas: Central, East, and West. World Showcase is located just south of Future World and hosts eleven country pavilions plus a few auxiliary areas in a loop around its lagoon.

The primary park entrance (for all intents and purposes the *Main Entrance*) is at the north end of Future World near the iconic Spaceship Earth (otherwise known as "*the big silver ball.*") This entrance has the main parking lot, bus drop off, and monorail station. There is a secondary entrance to the park that many tourists are blissfully unaware exists called the International Gateway. The International Gateway is situated between the country pavilions of France and the United Kingdom at the southwest corner of the park. This entrance allows access to the Epcot Area Resorts by footpath and also has *Friendship* boat service to the resorts and the Disney's Hollywood Studios theme park. The vast majority of guests arrive to Epcot via the Main Entrance, being deposited there by car, resort bus, or monorail.

Oh yes, the parking lot...

Depending on whom you ask Epcot's parking lot either has 11,391 spaces or room for 11,211 vehicles with grass areas to hold an additional 500+ vehicles. Regardless of which figure is accurate it is relatively huge at 141 acres. Please be sure to write down where you parked.

Supposedly the parking attendants can tell you roughly which section you parked in based on your time of arrival to the park, but there is doubt that even Disney is capable of pulling off such a miracle as to find your misplaced car before everyone else vacates the lots.

However, there is some statistical likelihood on their side. The parking lot has seven major sections and they tend to be parked in a predictable manner every day. The lots of **Imagine, Amaze,** and **Journey** are the three closest to the park entrance. **Imagine** is usually parked in the early morning hours prior to the park's typical 9 A.M. opening. Once the main influx of park guests begins to roll in **Amaze** and **Journey** will be parked. All of this allows Disney to not bother to run the tram until later in the morning. Yes, if you arrive early expect to walk to the park entrance. At least there is some attractive landscaping.

Directly behind those three smaller front lots and separated by a tree-lined drainage ravine are the larger **Explore, Create,** and **Discover** lots. **Explore** rarely gets parked unless the park is particularly busy. **Imagine** and **Explore** are situated to the east on a secondary tram line that only operates on the busiest days. **Create** and **Discover** are used on a typical park day and sit directly behind **Amaze** and **Journey** on the main tram line.

Depending on attendance projections **Create** and **Discover** will be parked at half, three-quarters, or full along the length of their lanes. This reduces the trek guests have to make from their parking space to the tram loading area when possible. However, this assumes the tram is even operating. Epcot is notorious for not running the tram at all during the slower periods, and when it does it's often only a single tram running to service the parking lot. Patience is a virtue.

Astute readers will have realized only six parking areas have been identified. There is a seventh – the ever mystical **Wonders** lot. Located on the second tier and to the far east with no front lot ahead of it, the **Wonders** lot lingers alone on the far end of the secondary tram line. If you parked there, expect to see Epcot busier than ever thought imaginable and give up all hope of riding the major headliner attractions. The **Wonders** parking lot is used for peak days like New Years Eve when the park attendance can swell to numbers north of 80,000 guests.

On that note, guests should be aware that the parking lot can and occasionally does reach capacity on those days with new arrivals being turned away. While flowing into the lot on the busiest of days is tightly controlled and runs relatively smoothly, exiting the parking lot can take upwards of two hours during the mass exodus after the nightly fireworks.

Speaking of the **Wonders** lot, there's a bit of irony in the naming of that rarely-used overflow lot. The lot was named after the Wonders of Life pavilion in Future World which opened in 1989. The pavilion is now defunct and used as a casual special events pavilion for a few weeks each year while otherwise sitting empty and abandoned. The lot was renamed along with the other lots of the parking area as the Wonders of Life was added to Future Word during a peak spike in the park's general attendance.

Now both are used infrequently and reflect the overall sagging attendance of the park as of late. Previously the parking lots were named as follows:

Rows 1-10 **Space (Journey)**, 11-25 **Energy (Discover)**, 26-38 **Harvest (Amaze)**, 39-54 **Communications (Create)**, 55-67 **Imagination (Imagine)**, 68-83 **Mobility (Explore)**, and 84-103 **Seas (Wonders)**.

Now if this parking lot discussion has not yet lulled you into a brief coma there are just a few more bits to touch on. Several rows at the front of **Amaze** lot are designated as handicap parking, with some overflow handicap spaces at the front of the **Journey** lot as well. There you will find *courtesy wheelchairs* to help guests with mobility issues in reaching the front of the park. These wheelchairs are parked between metal rails akin to shopping carts at a major chain grocery store and free to access by most anyone. The idea is that a guest with mobility issues who cannot traverse long distances on foot will park in the handicap section of the parking lot and then utilize one of these wheelchairs for the hike to the entrance of the park. Once inside the park, these guests would then either rent a wheelchair for the day or an *electronic convenience vehicle* as Disney calls them, known to every other person in the world as merely a power scooter.

That rarely happens as planned. Instead the wheelchairs are often pilfered by the curious ne'er-do-well and later found spread across the parking lot and occasionally in a drainage ravine. This is why the courtesy wheelchairs have little flags on poles so they can be found from a distance amid a sea of vehicles. Well, at least Disney tried.

On roads...

The parking lot is reasonably accessible from Walt Disney World's main roads of World Drive and Epcot Center Drive. Despite being somewhat debated, the best exit from Interstate 4 to reach the park is exit #67. Far more interesting though is the perimeter backstage road known as **Avenue of the Stars**.

Countless hours of really boring research with the public records office yields a surprising factoid: everything at Epcot is located somewhere on the road **Avenue of the Stars**. Also, there's nothing else on that road except for Epcot. So if someone happens to be looking through the records of the Orange County Comptroller's office and run across a building permit for *"Amazing new attraction installation at XYZ **Avenue of the Stars**"* then you know it's going to be for Epcot. But it's not like anyone actually sits around waiting anxiously for that particular permit to appear so they can post it immediately to the internet.

Assume you do discover an amazing building permit for *"XYZ **Avenue of the Stars**."* History has shown us that the permits Disney files are notoriously vague. How would you know where it is in the park? Check the address using this simple reference guide!

The addresses run around the park in a clockwise manner starting with the lowest number at the Front Entrance and/or East Gate Facility (awesome bathrooms, used to have a kennel – check it out sometime). All of the addresses have been culled from Notices of Commencement filed in the past few years.

Known Addresses on Avenue of the Stars

1310 - Epcot Front Entrance

1320 - Epcot Entrance / East Gate

1341 - Epcot Kennel (Defunct)

1360 - Flower/Garden Festival Hall (also known as Wonders of Life)

1365 - Imagineering Offices (Backstage)

1380 - Mission: SPACE

1400 - Raytheon Exhibit / Innoventions East (and Basement)

1404 - Epcot UV Fountain

1440 - Test Track VIP lounge

1446 - East Merchandise Shop

1478 - Duffy's Meet/Greet

1480 - San Angel Inn Restaurant / Mexico

1500 – Biergarten Restaurant

1510 - ATM location / Cast Services

1610 – Alfredo's Restaurant

1750 - Germany

1776 - American Gardens Theater

1779 - Tutto Italia Restaurant

1780 - Japan

1790 - Morocco

1830 - Chefs des France Restaurant

1920 - Canada

1982 - Refreshment Port

1990 - Imagination pavilion

2010 - Velcro Exhibit / The Land

2013 – The Land science internships office (Backstage)

2016 - EC trailer w-251 (Backstage)

2020 - Living Seas

2052 - Future World Restrooms East/West (likely Central)

2060 - Camera Center / Future World restrooms / Spaceship Earth

3. SPACESHIP EARTH

DOMINATING the park's skyline and looming over the entry plaza, the eighteen story tall silver geodesic sphere of the Spaceship Earth pavilion acts as an icon of the entire Epcot theme park.

Taking twenty-six months and 40,800 hours of labor the 165 foot diameter Spaceship Earth is an architectural monument in its own right. Rather than just being an extended dome structure (as originally planned) the building is a complete sphere. Previously such a structure was thought impossible as it was believed a complete sphere would collapse under its own weight. The ingenious design was accomplished by dividing the sphere into two main structural regions. The upper three-quarters of the sphere sit atop an elevated structural support ring. This ring is directly attached to the six massive legs of the main structure which are in turn driven deep into the earth for stability. This table-like structure supports both the upper dome atop it as well as the lower quarter of the total-sphere which hangs down beneath it. The entire sphere is thus suspended eighteen feet off the ground.

Held at a distance of about three feet off the main structure is the silver alucobond paneling that gives Spaceship Earth its distinctive look. There are 11,324 triangular facets in total. Between these panels is a gap of spacing which allows for a gutter system. The system captures the rainfall on the building and redirects the flow into the World Showcase lagoon rather than allowing it to fall over the sides of the sphere as a deluge onto the attraction queue.

The alucobond skin itself was designed to diffusely reflect the landscape surrounding Spaceship Earth. The panels were intended to be self cleaning (by way of rainfall) and feature a surface smoother than glass. However, the sphere is actually cleaned on a schedule by maintenance workers rappelling down from the top and power washing the structure at night. There is an access panel on the top of the sphere to accomplish this task.

Home to a staple attraction of the park experience lineup since the grand opening, Spaceship Earth has been ever-present but constantly in flux. Created as the communication themed pavilion, the ride within Spaceship Earth tells the history of mankind as we evolve and grow our ability to communicate. Communication was considered a central theme of the entire Epcot concept. As stated at the Spaceship Earth pavilion dedication ceremony by Card Walker: *"communications is the beginning of understanding and thus fitting of the park's marquee attraction."*

Conceptually speaking, Spaceship Earth has always been a slow-moving thirteen minute omnimover attraction with blue four person vehicles and an integrated headrest audio system. Original plans for the pavilion had the main show scenes housed in the building just south of a large faceted dome. The original planned dome was to contain an extended version of the star-filled finale akin to what exists at the top of the sphere today. Luckily for the world the dome became a complete sphere as the entire ride was moved to be housed inside it. This resulted in the familiar corkscrew spiral of show scenes culminating in the planetarium star field followed by a brief (and steep) backwards return to earth through the sphere's core.

Some show scenes have been revised over the years but the same basic flow of scenes remains. Every version of the ride has begun with a steep incline from the **Loading Area** into the sphere. This space has often been referred to as a **Time Tunnel** or **Vortex**. At the top of this lift hill the vehicles would formally be on the lowest of three levels within the sphere in the northeastern quadrant.

Upon leveling out the first major scene of the ride introduced guests to the **Prehistoric Period** with a projection of a wooly mammoth with the narration emphasis on the need of man to work in collaborative groups. This large projection screen would wrap around the side of the vehicle track as it made a u-turn to follow the spiral path upward around the sphere's perimeter. It transitioned into an actual **Cave Scene** populated with a realistically styled group of cave-people drawing cave paintings – a first record of shared information. Better ways to record information eventually evolved and the vehicles enter into an **Egyptian Temple**. They pass a slave pounding out papyrus paper and further ahead a Pharaoh dictates to a scribe. Once being recorded, information needs to be shared. **Phoenician Merchants** in the next scene on their boats out at sea trade information between them. They are cited with creating a common alphabet so different cultures can communicate. This starlit vignette ends the first tier of the sphere.

Passing under a grand stone archway the guest vehicles glide into the second tier and a scene of **Greek Scholars** where the sharing of information flourishes (either theater or mathematics depending on the ride version). Fluted columns rise up around the vehicles giving way to a **Roman Roads** scene illustrating the vast expanse of shared knowledge. In the next scene **Rome Burns** as guests see its embers and information is lost. A suitably smoky scent is pumped in to the scene. All is not lost though as **Jewish and Arabic Scholars** around the corner have their libraries of knowledge safely stored away. Similarly in a cathedral **Abbey Monks** toil endlessly copying information by hand. Obviously there must be an easier way and thus the **Gutenberg Press** is invented. Knowledge once again flourishes as highlighted by painters, sculptors and musicians of the **Renaissance** surround the vehicles. The second tier is finished with a dramatic climb up toward Michelangelo lying on his back painting the ceiling of the **Sistine Chapel**.

The ride jumps ahead several hundred years to the industrial revolution where a **Steam Press** prints newspapers en masse. New technology for communication grows through a rapid series of vignettes: the **Telegraph**, **Telephone**, **Radio** and **Cinema**. On a more personal level and closer to home a family watches **Television**. The next few scenes on the third tier have changed for nearly every version of the attraction. They have all generally referred to modern technological advances and computers though.

Just before entering the top of the sphere and the planetarium, the vehicles ride through a **Data Flow** tunnel meant to replicate the dramatic flow of information and acceleration of knowledge sharing speed. They then emerge into the Spaceship Earth **Planetarium** surrounded by the open space of the domed roof of the sphere with thousands of stars projected onto the walls and a view of Earth, as seen from space, in the distance. The vehicles then rotate 180° and travel down backward into the central core of the building through infinite stars and the ever-changing **Descent Tunnel** which leads to the **Unload Area**. Afterward guests exit into the attach building's post-show area – originally meant to house the ride itself. Many aspects of the attraction have remained the same since it opened in 1982, but there have been three major overhauls so far in its history.

1982-1986: The Original

The original opening day version of Spaceship Earth was sponsored by Bell System and narrated by Vic Perrin (some say it was Larry Dobkin). While still containing many of the core show scenes we equate with the ride today, the attraction lacked a musical score and the narration was very dry. Some went as far as to call it boring. The original script was a group effort on the part of Imagineering and Ray Bradbury with research compiled by Peggie Fariss from the Smithsonian Institute, the Huntington Library, and the Universities of Chicago and Southern California. The book reference list alone was nineteen pages long. Sadly, enthralling dramatic writers they as a group were not.

Just prior to the **Data Flow** tunnel was a large scene known as the **Network Communication Map**. A group of animatronic figures tended to computers below a large illuminated glass map of the Bell System data network. The **Planetarium** star field featured imagery of astronauts in space. A striking scene involved a young girl looking out the window of a space station above the ride path as it entered into the central core. She was watching a robotic arm and astronauts suspended over the ride path attempting to repair a satellite.

The finale itself was a hazy backward journey down from the **Planetarium** star field with screens showing satellite imagery, nanotechnology, thermal imaging, and computer graphics of communications advances while an audio loop of communications chatter played. At best it was clinically factual; at worst it was painfully dull. Unlike the other three versions, no one seems to support the original Spaceship Earth as their favorite version of the attraction. Regardless the ride did get over 7.5 million riders in the first year of operation with over 100,000 guest rides recorded in less than a week of its opening.

Highlights from the 1982 ride narration:

PERRIN: Where have we come from, where are we going? The answers begin in our past. In the dust from which we were formed, answers recorded on the walls of time. So let us journey into that past, to seek those walls, to know ourselves and to probe the destiny of our Spaceship Earth.

PERRIN: Poised on the threshold of infinity, we see our world as it truly is: small, silent, fragile, alive, a drifting island in the midnight sky. It is our spaceship. Our Spaceship Earth.

PERRIN: Now our future world draws near -and we face the challenge of tomorrow. We must return and take command of our Spaceship Earth. To become captains of our own destiny. To reach out and fulfill our dreams.

Earth Station

The original post-show area design shared by the first two versions of the main ride was called **Earth Station**. It functioned as Epcot's guest relations area – thought to be a sort of futuristic town square. The area had six 6' x 14' rear projection screens along the top perimeter of the space. They showed an abstract film about the various attractions in the park. Each screen originally had 1,008 diffusion panels giving them a mosaic effect. A central seventh screen had park news and updates changing throughout the day. **Earth Station** had two guest relations desks for things like reservations and park information.

It was also the home of numerous **World Key** information kiosks. **World Key** was developed in collaboration by Bell System and Disney. Each kiosk featured a touch screen directory of Epcot that would offer information about the park pulled from laser discs. It also allowed guests to connect in a video chat with a guest relations cast member to make reservations at the numerous park restaurants or ask questions. **Earth Station** housed ten of the park's twenty-nine **World Key** screens. The others were located in **CommuniCore** and an outpost at the Germany pavilion.

1986-1994: Tomorrow's Child

Bell System underwent structural reorganization within the company in the early 1980s. AT&T prevailed as the marquee brand and would be promoted via a revitalized Spaceship Earth experience. The ride closed for four days in May of 1986 to switch over to the next iteration. Mentions of the outdated sponsor branding were replaced. A new narrator was brought on board in the form of television personality Walter Cronkite. The script itself underwent mostly cosmetic changes at the hand of Imagineering's Tom Fitzgerald to be a bit more dramatic and interesting, while the attraction's show scenes mostly remained physically the same.

Two computer scenes were added with the **Personal Computer** and **Paperless Office** scenes placed just before the entry tunnel to the **Planetarium** star field. Both of these scenes featured animatronics relocated from other parts of the ride: the **Personal Computer** was attended by a figure which used to work on the **Printing Press** and the **Paperless Office** was manned by a woman pulled from the **Network Communications Map**. A voice-over reminder was added in the pre-planetarium tunnel to warn riders that their vehicles would rotate backwards in the coming scene. The most significant difference was a full score added to the ride-through as well as an overall theme song in the form of "Tomorrow's Child."

"Tomorrow's Child" was a two-part song written by Ron Ovadia and Peter Stougaard. The song was introduced to riders as an instrumental during the **Planetarium** star field then would blossom into the full song sung by Sally Stevens during the remaining **Descent** portion. The visual effects on the screens in the **Descent** were modified to

22

better fit the song, and mirrored wall panels in the final portion were enhanced with lighting to give a sense of infinite depth around the vehicles. The "Tomorrow's Child" song gave an uplifting ending to the attraction, introducing the idea that today's children will be tomorrow's explorers and leaders.

In the **Earth Station** post show area the mosaic-style diffusion elements over the projection screens were removed. The central overhead screen was replaced with a panel that had a UV lit Epcot flower logo. The exact date of these changes is unclear, but it was complete by the 1986 ride renovation.

Highlights of the 1986 ride narration:

CRONKITE: For eons, our planet has drifted as a spaceship through the universe. And for a brief moment, we have been its passengers. Yet in that time, we've made tremendous progress in our ability to record and share knowledge. So let's journey back 40,000 years to the dawn of recorded history. .

STEVENS: Tomorrow's child, tomorrow's child, shining a brand new way, for the future world is born today.

CRONKITE: Yes, Tomorrow's Child, embodying our hopes and dreams for the future. A future made possible by the information age. The technologies of this new era will extend our reach, expand the capabilities of the human mind and help us shape a better tomorrow.

1994-2007: Flood of Babble

AT&T decided to renew their sponsorship contract for Spaceship Earth and the ride underwent further upgrades. This new version opened on November 23, 1994. The Tomorrow's Child song was removed from the attraction and the ride-through was entirely rescored by Edo Guidotti. The tone of the ride changed as Jeremy Irons narrated a more dramatic script once again penned by Tom Fitzgerald. The entire attraction took on a somewhat heavier moody and reflective atmosphere.

Major scenic changes were made in the final approach to the **Planetarium** star field and the remainder of the ride from that point forward. The **Network Communication Map** scene was entirely removed, and the **Personal Computer** scenes with the boy in his bedroom and the woman in her **Paperless Office** were replaced with a single large scene of two young people video chatting. **Jason and Kaiko** communicated via an intelligent videophone program that automatically translated their speech into each other's language. Jason was located somewhere in the USA (likely California because of his surf board ownership) while Kaiko was in Japan with a gorgeous UV-lit tree full of cherry blossoms behind her. The data flew back and forth across the ocean between them by fiber optic special effect.

All references to actual spaceships or space travel were removed from the **Planetarium** star field. The scene of a girl looking out of the space station window at astronauts on a spacewalk was removed, the space station portion itself painted over in black. A screen went up in the area just prior to the first decline of the descent showing the interconnectedness of modern technology through cycling

Global News Reports. At the first decline itself where the space station used to be featured a new laser effect would create patterned beams that seemed to envelope the ride vehicles. A **Virtual Classroom** scene was added into the descent, showing students and a teacher working with a program together in a group with other classrooms around the world. The area previously populated by abstractly shaped rear-projection screens for the "Tomorrow's Child" sequence was replaced with **Star Fields**. These effects were made of slowly spinning armatures with tiny point lights.

The remainder of the descent focused on a series of **Video-Phone Vignettes** sharing important moments across the world with flashes of fiber optic special effects. A mother sang a lullaby to her daughter from miles away, a family celebrated a graduation ceremony for their daughter that they couldn't physically attend, and a scientist excitedly shared his fossil discovery with a colleague. The vignettes culminated in a large set piece of a dazzling **Futuristic City** that lit up with fiber optics effects. This city had bands of fiber optics that stretched out and expanded to create a **Canopy** that engulfed the ride vehicles overhead. The **Canopy** was full of color changing fiber optic light points that washed over the vehicles in waves in synch with the attraction's score.

It would be beneficial at this point to discuss the finer details of the 1994 renovation's score. The score was based on Bach's Sinfonia n° 2 in C Minor, specifically the variation used by Isao Tomita in "The Sea Named Solaris" which is where the ocean-waves-crashing motif originates from. Imagery of waves of inspiration and a flood of electronic babble in the narration reinforce this overarching theme of the 1994 revision.

Highlights of the 1994 ride narration:

IRONS: Like a grand and miraculous spaceship, our planet has sailed through the universe of time. And for a brief moment, we have been among its many passengers. From the very beginning, we have always sought to reach out to one another...to bridge the gaps between us... to communicate.

IRONS: But will these seemingly infinite communications become a flood of electronic babble? Or will we use this power to usher in a new age of understanding and co-operation on this, our Spaceship Earth.

IRONS: Since the dawn of recorded time, communication has revolutionized our lives and changed our world. We now have the ability and the responsibility to build new bridges of acceptance and co-operation between us; to create a better world for ourselves and our children as we continue our amazing journey aboard Spaceship Earth.

Global Neighborhood

In the post-show a newly themed area called **Global Neighborhood** replaced **Earth Station**. The **World Key** kiosks and **Guest Relations** elements moved to the northeast corner of the nearby **CommuniCore** building allowing the ride to have its own real post-show area. The main component of the **Global Neighborhood** was the **Ride the AT&T Network** simulator. Guests would step onto a domed platform that would tilt from side to side in-synch with a video showing the rapid constant flow of information. Other elements flanking the space focused on technology AT&T was hoping to develop for consumers. **You Don't Say** featured automatic translation technology. **Communication Breakthrough** would have guests playing a sort of pong styled game with a video phone. **Storyteller Phone** allowed guests to make phone calls while creating false background ambiance to give the impression they were calling from exotic locals. **Interactive Wonderland** had guests step into a booth with a bench seat simulating a small home living room environment. There they would interact with a television that took voice commands to tell an interactive story based on the characters of Disney's televised live-action *Alice in Wonderland* series which was popular at the time.

In 1999 the **Global Neighborhood** would be renovated into the **New Global Neighborhood**. **Ride the AT&T Network** would be removed and replaced with a **Network Tree** that sprouted from the center of the space. The tree was metallic and featured glowing fiber optic cables integrated into its structure. The tree featured holes in the trunk where guests could put their face and have their picture taken – these photos would then be featured on various screens hanging from the branches of the tree. The remaining exhibits of the space were unchanged until 2003 when AT&T's sponsorship ended and portions of the post-show were simply closed without replacement for several years.

2007-Present: Fresh Overtones

In January of 2003 AT&T opted not to renew its expiring sponsorship of the Spaceship Earth pavilion.

References to the company were subsequently removed from the attraction. In November of 2005 Siemens signed on as the new sponsor of the attraction. After much planning, the ride closed on July 9, 2007, to begin its transformation into the attraction we know today, beginning soft opening in December 2007 and grand opening in February of 2008. The attraction was fully rescored by Bruce Broughton and narrated by Dame Judy Dench. It featured a script that reached for something broader than just communications to the idea of each generation of mankind creating the future for the next.

The ride vehicles were removed from the structure in groups and fitted with a touch screen interface for each row of passengers. The initial **Ascent** had its safety warning films which were added late in the life of the 1994 version removed. This area was now used to introduce the new interactive screens. Passengers would select the language for their ride narration, denote their home location on a map of the world, and then smile for a trackside camera which took a picture of passenger's faces before they were returned to **Spaceship Earth Control** and entered into the first of the ride's show scenes.

The **Prehistoric** scene was changed from a slide projection format to a full motion video sequence projection on the large screen. Animated cave painting projections were added around the **Cave** scene. Many props and set pieces were replaced or refurbished. Several scenes were restaged. A figure from the **Renaissance** scene moved into the spectator group of the **Greek** scene. The **Greek** scene changed themes from theatrical performance to astronomy lecture. **James and Kaiko's** video conference was entirely removed and replaced, with James joining the family in the prior family **Television** scene.

Throughout the ride the lighting and sound systems were upgraded. The animatronics were all given limb refurbishments and their major movements updated to compliance standards. This technology smoothed out and minimized the jerky motions earlier model animatronics were known for. Major figures in the attraction were changed to fully compliant A-100 figures to give them broader range of motion and greater realism.

A new series of scenes was added just before the **Planetarium** star field entry tunnel. The new **Early Computer** scene featured the female character from the **Radio** show scene relocated and dressed in go-go boots and a lab coat. She was now a scientist surrounded by banks of a tape data mainframe along with a new male counterpart. Next, a scene depicting a **Suburban Garage** with a young man assembling his own personal computer was added. The **Data Flow** tunnel leading into the **Planetarium** was completely overhauled and now consists of a projection screen tube around the vehicles instead of a solid tunnel with attached lighting effects.

After the **Planetarium** star field, the vehicles enter into a seemingly **Endless Grid** of blue points of light. The **News Feed**, laser, and **Virtual Classroom** were all removed. The original space station's outline can be made out in the rear of the endless blue grid. The touch screens in the vehicles turn on and ask the passengers some basic preference questions. The questions are used to formulate a video sequence based on the individual choices of each set of passengers. This video sequence plays for each passenger set according to their preferences and by inserting the passengers' faces onto figures to show a personalized version of *"Your Future."* All other show scenes were removed entirely and simple blue triangular panels flank certain portions of the **Descent**. The focus of the rider is intended to be on the screen in the vehicle itself.

Highlights of the 2007 ride narration:

DENCH: Remember how easy it was to learn your ABCs? Thank the Phoenicians. They invented them.

DENCH: Young people with a passion for shaping the future put the power of the computer in everyone's hands. Once again we stand on the brink of a new Renaissance.

DENCH: After 30,000 years of time travel here we are. A truly global community: networked, online, poised to shape the future of Spaceship Earth.

Project Tomorrow

The post-show area of the attraction would become **Project Tomorrow** under Siemens. The area opened in phases with two games opening in December of 2007 and two more opening in January of 2008. The main feature of the redesigned space is a large illuminated globe which pinpoints the location-choice of guests from the ride. Each chosen point on the map glows as the guests exit the attraction and the mass of glowing spots grows throughout the operational day. **Body Builder** is a 3D game that allows guests to assemble a digital human body that emphasizes remote controlled health technology. **Super Driver** is a driving simulation in a smart car with computerized collision avoidance systems. **Power City** is a large shuffle-board like game where power units are moved to develop areas on a projected interactive map. **Inner Vision** is meant to be a futuristic medical diagnostic tool.

It should be noted that the latest version of Spaceship Earth is not without its critics. Despite an overall approval for the improvements made to the audio-animatronics figures in the attraction the use of the touch screens and the new ride finale have been less well received by the public. For all its technological innovation, the touch screen setup as it exists at Spaceship Earth is criticized for being implemented as a throw-away gimmick. While the screens could be used to provide information, subtitles, or even captioning throughout the ride they are only used for the brief ascent and descent portions. It almost seems like an abrupt misuse of the technology.

Further, the actual finale of the ride is entirely on the screen. The scenery of the ride's finale in previous versions focused on beautifully lit set pieces and fiber optic effects around the vehicles. There's no arguing that the descent of the attraction is a tightly cramped location and that getting scenery into the space is difficult at best – but the previous versions did have scenery, thus proving it could be done. The current version of the ride has black curtains and the occasional exposed bit of ride or building infrastructure visible to passengers. If a guest looks up from their in-vehicle video they will notice they are traveling through a space that was half-finished at best. Assuming that guests simply wouldn't notice an area as unfinished was not Disney's policy in the past, so one can hope it is not their stance going forward. Perhaps it will be reconsidered in the future as the original 1982 Spaceship Earth finale was redone after four years because its ending was found lacking as well.

4. UNIVERSE OF ENERGY

THERE IS nothing unintentional about the seemingly over-simplistic square design of the Universe of Energy pavilion. Originally envisioned as a solar energy pavilion complete with parabolic collector, the design of the pavilion began to take on its present shape and location when Exxon signed-on as the sponsor. Under Exxon, the lauding of solar energy for the future would become just one of many *energy alternatives* the company wanted to present within the pavilion. Photovoltaic cells on the roof, in the form of 2,156 solar panels, were decided on as a means to incorporate the ideals of solar energy into the decidedly now more diverse pavilion.

This meant that careful consideration of the shape and location of the building would be needed in order for those cells to properly collect light. A careful study determined the track of the sun over the proposed park. The pavilion's

105,000 square foot structure became firmly anchored in the northern portion of Future World East facing southward and tilted thirty degrees off horizontal. Subsequently, this off-kilter plunging design lent itself to a sense of visual kinetic energy as the pavilion rose from its apex which has been driven down into the ground. Starting at just twenty feet above the entrance to the pavilion the roof rises up to sixty feet at the rear.

The motifs of the square and the grid would be reused multiple times throughout the pavilion. Seen from the air the pavilion is almost a perfect square. The façade was embellished with 180,000 square mirrors and the reflecting pool would be lined with similarly sized blue tiles. The original exterior paint scheme of the pavilion fading from a deep red, to orange and finally to yellow, suggested the notion of radiating energy. The planters at the front corners of the pavilion were originally smaller reflecting pools in the same style as the main pool. Though some elements of the design have been lost since the 1996 refurbishment, the overall aesthetic design remains largely what it was when the pavilion debuted.

1982-1996: The Original

Crossing the threshold into the building through either one of a pair of double sliding glass doors guests would find themselves facing a long tiled wall. This wall, the **Thermal Mosaic**, presents a thermal image of the sun with the earth depicted in proper proportion as a tiny white dot on the right side of the mural. The mural was designed to immediately present guests with an idea of the immense power of our sun. It also informed them of the current wait for the next pre-show film through embedded glass block tiles behind which an illuminated pre-show countdown timer was displayed.

The 500 person standing-room **Pre-Show** theater contained a screen 90' x 14' composed of one hundred rotating 3½ foot square elements. Each block had alternating black and white faces along with the ability to rotate to show any of these faces individually or an angled combination thereof. This technological wonder and its stunning effect wouldn't be functional until the middle of 1984, nearly two years after the Universe of Energy had begun daily operation. Until it was finally running reliably, the blocks were each turned to show only their white face masquerading as a simple projection screen.

The original pre-show film, known as the *Kinetic Mosaic*, was envisioned by Czech artist and director Emil Radok. As the film began the screen would ripple to life, spinning different panels to match the projected imagery. Each individual panel had its own microprocessor to control its movement. Over a billion different combinations of the screen elements were possible. The effect was mesmerizing and considered by many to be more engrossing than the main show beyond. The long continuous screen effect was made possible by projecting five 35mm films running in unison. The films subject matter dealt with atomic, chemical, electrical, mechanical, heat and light energy and man's harnessing of each for his own use. The film concluded by posing the challenge for mankind to find alternative energy sources for the future. This included the song "Energy (You Make the World Go 'Round)" performed by Bob Moline.

MOLINE: Energy, these are a few of your faces, glowing in timeless places. Bringing our lives new graces. Energy, there is no living without you, we must keep learning about you. Now is the time to find how to. Energy, you are profound, you make the world go 'round and 'round.

As the song ended the lights would rise and the doors into the main theater located underneath the pre-show screen would open beckoning guests forward.

Theater I

It's important to note at this junction that the Universe of Energy was and is still a forty-five minute presentation that begins with the eight minute pre-show film. The remaining thirty-seven minutes is inside the massive traveling-theater vehicles. These vehicles start unassumingly in the first theater, **Theater I**, in a large six-pack configuration with a pair of ramps from the rear doors allowing guests to enter the vehicles. Most guests don't notice the gentle slope up into the vehicles. Since the ramps are level with the floor of the vehicles they assume they've entered a typical theater with bench seating. Unbeknownst to most guests, the six 97-passenger vehicles were already sitting atop a large air powered turntable as the show began.

The show design was deceptively simple but managed a stunning effect. Guests entering from the rear would cross directly under a 32' x 155' projection screen that few looked behind themself to notice. Once seated in the vehicle there were facing floor to ceiling shimmering theatrical curtains. These curtains angled in from the sides, matching the shape of the theater space itself, to a smallish curtained panel at the apex of the room. Most guests assumed this curtain would open and the show would begin on a relatively small screen. Instead as the show began the lights would go out in the theater and the turntable would inflate and rotate the vehicle around 180 degrees to face the massive main screen.

In **Theater I** guests would watch the four and a half minute animated film called the *Energy Creation Story*, directed by veteran Disney animator Jack Boyd. As with other films shown at EPCOT Center at the time, the images were projected at thirty frames per second. This was opposed to the standard twenty-four frames per second in order to eliminate any possible projection flutter. The film showed guests the dawn of life on Earth and how sunlight gave rise to microscopic creatures that fed on tiny plants that captured energy from the sun. It went on to explain how these creatures eventually died and formed a layer of organic matter which was compressed over millions of years into shale, and finally into oil and gas. The film concluded with a fierce thunderstorm in a prehistoric marsh as dinosaurs ran for cover.

> **NARRATOR:** Much of the Earth's present supply was deposited during the primeval era when great reptiles roamed the land. Come with us now and experience a few moments from that dark and mysterious past.

At this point the airbags of the turntable under the vehicles would again inflate to turn the vehicles ninety degrees to the left to face the side wall of the theater. The movement was synchronized to the film wrapping off the screen so it was at first barely noticeable. The curtain covering the side wall of the theater would rise up partially while a massive hydraulic door lowered into the ground to reveal the **Primeval Diorama** in the distance. Much to the average guest's surprise, the vehicles would slowly move forward and into a large holding area within the **Primeval Diorama**. Once situated, the large hydraulic door behind the vehicles would rise up from the floor and seal off the diorama area from the light and sound bleed from the adjacent theater.

Fun facts: At this point the **Theater I** operator is sitting alone in the dark in the massive theater space at the ride's primary control console. This console is located just underneath the left side of the main show screen. Now empty of vehicles, the turntable realigns itself to match the vehicle path at the other side of the theater. Within moments the curtains on the other side of the space would rise, the hydraulic wall would lower, and the second set of ride vehicles would return to **Theater I** to conclude their journey and unload. The four show doors within the attraction are twelve feet tall, roughly one foot thick, and can be as wide as ninety-two feet. Their movement is a sight most guests never experience as they fail to look behind themselves during the attraction.

The Universe of Energy has thirteen ride vehicles. There are the primary twelve, making up the two standard six-pack formations, and a spare. These vehicles are commonly referred to as traveling theater units. They are self-propelled and self-powered with eight lead-acid automotive batteries on-board each vehicle. The vehicles move individually and are free-roaming. To stay on course the vehicles listen for a radio signal from a one-eighth inch guide-wire embedded in the concrete of the floor. There is no track, though one may see wheel paths on the floor. These paths have had the carpet removed in order to lower the amount of static electricity built up by the traveling theater vehicles, which in the early days would constantly fry their onboard computers.

The vehicle batteries are charged by charging plates on the turntables located in each theater. There are no exposed electrical connections and no actual physical contact between the vehicles and the plates. Powerful electromagnets located within the charging plates interact with magnetic coils located on the underside of the vehicles inducing an electrical current. The charging plates are partially powered by the solar array on the roof of the building. The array is capable of generating approximately 77 kilowatts of DC electrical current, allowing guests to *"ride on sunshine"* through the attraction.

Primeval Diorama

The original design of the **Primeval Diorama** was meant to convey nearly 300 million years of prehistory in a short seven minute ride-through. It begins in the **Carboniferous Period** as the vehicles roll into the large holding area filled with low laying fog. A shallow pond directly ahead is filled with a family of Brontosaurus (Apatosaurus). One dinosaur leans forward to investigate the vehicles while the others casually munch on plants. A few Edaphosaurus can be seen directly to the right amid the trees. The vehicles begin to break away into a single file line to enter the main diorama scenes.

The front left vehicle leads the pack and turns a sharp left into the diorama. Almost immediately the scenery jumps over one hundred million years and the vehicles have entered the early **Jurassic Period**. Trachodons and a small waterfall are to the left and a Stegosaurus and

Allosaurus battle on a rocky outcropping straight ahead. The outcroppings become unstable and large rocks are teetering overhead amid intense geologic activity as guests enter the **Cretaceous Period**. A family of Ornithomimus watch helplessly as one is trapped in a bubbling mud pit, doomed by the hostile environment. A large snake-like Elasmosaurus lashes out toward the vehicle as Pteranodons loom overhead. A violent **Volcanic Eruption** directly ahead threatens to envelop the entire scene and bring about mass extinction. The vehicles enter a cavern at the base of the volcano and amid a cloud of fog arrive in the quiet confines of a darkened **Theater II** where the vehicles regroup into their six-pack configuration.

The elaborate scenery of the **Primeval Diorama** includes more than 250 prehistoric trees, some of which are more than forty feet tall. A lightweight foam plastic with molecular characteristics similar to the cellulose structure of a plant's wood pulp was used to create the vegetation. This plastic gave the trees the ability to sway realistically in the wind created by massive blower fans. The mural behind the marsh scene is 515 feet in length and 32 feet tall. It took over 6,000 man hours to paint and was specially crafted for the day-to-night transitional effects that are shone upon it.

There are twenty-six animatronic creatures included in the diorama including giant snails and dueling millipedes. The distinct swampy smell was provided by a Disney smellitizer machine providing a scent formulation known as damp earth. Special effects include an ever-recycling flow of lava made essentially from gelatin and black-light pigment. A large fountain with lighting effects sits above the cave into **Theater II** to splash the spewing magma of the volcano.

Theater II

Upon entering **Theater II** the guests aboard the traveling theater vehicles would be returned to the present timeframe and see a large set piece directly ahead known as the **EPCOT Energy Information Center**. Television monitors and a series of three large illuminated glass maps of the world showed different forms of energy from all over the world in s pseudo-monitoring station setup. Effectively this was all an elaborate way to disguise the **Theater II** operations console as part of the set. There was a brief explanatory narration that played while the vehicles regrouped atop the turntable.

NARRATOR: These monitors behind the operating console show current and future energy resources around the world. Among them are: fossil fuels, nuclear, hydroelectric, geothermal, wind, and solar. Your Traveling Theatre vehicles are partially powered by the sun. The solar cells on this building's roof help recharge batteries in the vehicles when they're stopped. Computers guide the vehicles along a wire that is just an eighth of an inch thick! The maps highlight locations we'll visit during the next part of our journey.

Once the vehicles were all situated the show door would rise and close-off the diorama and the left-side projection screen would lower into place with the other two large format screens to cover the hydraulic door. The vehicles would rotate around to face the screens and watch a twelve and half minute film. The three massive 70mm motion projection screens together formed a giant wraparound screen that measured 210 feet wide and 30 feet high. It created a 218 degree field-of-view designed to extend beyond the viewers' peripheral vision. The film itself focused on man's quest for energy sources and the lengths he would go to recover them. Eventually the film concluded with a space shuttle launch in which the three screens rose into the air to allow the vehicles to move forward underneath them and back into **Theater I**.

Finale

The return to **Theater I** was made more fantastical by the chameleon properties of the space. The large curtains flanking the room would now be drawn up to the ceiling to reveal the side walls were completely covered in mirrors. The apex screen at the front of the theater was also now revealed – a convex half-cylindrical shaped 35mm projection screen. Together with the primary 70mm screen used earlier in the introduction, the films created the effect of a full-surround projection as it reflected off the mirrors.

The finale presented the idea of what was possible from energy. Mankind was discovering how energy was an ever-present force that filled every action and reaction, no matter how small. The screen at the front of the theater acted as the source of energy being exerted while the three giant screens along the rear wall of the theater acted as the environment affected. Full of bright lights and glowing colors the scenes morphed from one image to another in an interpretive progression. The two minute film sequence directed by David Moore used cutting-edge computer graphics of the day. The mirror reflection effect created the sense of 300 feet of continuous space flanking out around the vehicles. During the sequence the vehicles would rotate back to their starting position to prepare for unload. The spectacle was accompanied by the song "Universe of Energy" written by Al Kasha and Joel Hirschhorn.

SINGER: Feel the flow, here we go, through the Universe of Energy. Feel it grow, see it glow, it's the Universe of Energy.

The song concluded and the curtains would fall, revealing the guests were actually back where they began their journey. The automated doors would open to the rear left and allow guests to exit the pavilion. The Universe of Energy had no formal post-show, but rather dedicated space in nearby **CommuniCore** known as **The Energy Exchange.**

1996-Present: Ellen's Energy Adventure

By the early 1990s the content of the original show was starting to become outdated and inaccurate. Further, guest feedback was showing a troubling trend of regarding the attraction as overly serious and stale. Based on their success with humor as mode of delivery in nearby pavilions, Imagineering decided humor and satire was to be the approach for a revamped Universe of Energy. *Ellen's Energy Crisis* was to be hosted by comedian Ellen DeGeneres, along with television personality Bill Nye, the science guy.

The original show closed on January 21, 1996. The pavilion's interior was revamped and ready for the new show by mid-June, but the filming of the show was still incomplete in California. It was decided that the original Universe of Energy would reopen in the modified pavilion to help ease crowds at the park. The hybrid show ran with the old films but several physical elements missing until September when it closed again, to reopen on September 15, 1996, as *Ellen's Energy Crisis*. The ride operated for two weeks while receiving tweaks and edits to the films from Imagineering including a last-minute name change to *Ellen's Energy Adventure* before the grand opening on October 1, 1996.

The Radok screens in the pre-show were initially to be reused but later revisions of the Ellen script eventually had them replaced with five new stretched screens covering the same space. The pre-show audio system, hidden behind the screens, was entirely replaced and the projectors received upgrades. New lighting was added to illuminate the screens between shows in a wash of color since they could no longer turn to black panels when not in use. A small stage was added to the front of the space to allow cast members to deliver spiels along with the new show.

The new **Pre-Show** film focused on the exploits of Ellen as she falls asleep on her couch watching her college rival, Judy (Jamie Lee Curtis), playing *Jeopardy* on television. As Ellen points out, anyone who falls asleep while watching television will of course have a dream sequence. This dream sequence quickly devolves into a nightmare in which Ellen is on *Jeopardy* against Judy and Albert Einstein and all of the questions are about energy. Ellen begins to lose badly. However, Ellen soon realizes she is in a dream, seizes control, and calls on her neighbor, Bill Nye the Science Guy to help her win the game in the second round. Bill tells Ellen he will have to teach her about energy and they will start by going back to the beginning. The pre-show doors then open into **Theater I**, where the dream is set to continue.

In **Theater I** the sparkling original show curtains have been replaced with deep navy curtains. Beneath the main three screens two giant subwoofers have been installed to further the effect of the show. The ride follows the same movement as the original show, turning to face the screens. The new subwoofers create a near-deafening experience as the big bang creation of the universe is depicted on screen. The end of the sequence lands Ellen and Bill in the prehistoric period, which transitions to the **Diorama** much like the original show.

New foliage was planted throughout the **Diorama** making it greener and less rocky than the original. The dinosaurs were given new skins reflecting updated theories on the coloring of dinosaur flesh. They were repainted from their original deep green, brown and gray colors to almost florescent shades of green, orange, blue and yellow. A water misting sneeze-effect was added to one Brontosaurus who overhangs the vehicle path from the family pool. The Ornithomimus who had been drowning and flailing in the original show was also given a water effect to spit into the passing vehicles as he sits apparently unfazed in a pool of water. The smellitizers were deactivated during the renovation and the damp earth and volcano scents were lost.

The most noticeable change is the addition of an Ellen Degeneres animatronic to battle the Elasmosaurus in the **Tidal Pool**. The million dollar third generation animatronic ironically looks very little like Ellen to most guests but does feature extremely lifelike movements. During the partial-transition-opening the Ellen character was hidden behind a large rock. The **Diorama** also received all new audio tracks for the dinosaur sound effects, as well as a new musical score.

In **Theater II** the **EPCOT Energy Information Center** set was entirely demolished and removed. All that remains is the operations console, which is now hidden at the base of a large black-lit radio tower image. A simple plywood panel painted black was placed in front of the consol to disguise its original futuristic design and allow it to blend into the background.

During the transitional opening of the attraction the audio for **Theater II** had to be reworked to remove all reference to the **EPCOT Energy Information Center**. Twinkling lighting effects were added to the space to allow the vehicles to enter the theater in a sort of snowy haze befitting the theme of the new scene. Additionally, new black reveal curtains were installed to hide the side-flanking screens of the show. At the proper point in the show they would open on Ellen's command to reveal the full scope of the projection space.

The new **Theater II** sequence begins with the vehicles regrouping in the twinkling light pools as the radio tower broadcasts **KNRG News Radio** from the ice age. It then transitions to the main **Theater II** film in which Ellen is brought to the site of various energy sources by Bill Nye. This results in Ellen returning to *Jeopardy* with a head full of new knowledge which she uses to sweep *Double Jeopardy* and catch up to her nemesis Judy. The film sequence culminates in *Final Jeopardy*, where the screen rises as the game show's iconic theme plays. The two remaining contestants, Ellen and Judy, ponder the *Final Jeopardy* Clue:

ALEX TREBEK: This is the one source of power that will never run out.

For the new finale, the three main screens of **Theater I** now continue the *Final Jeopardy* sequence begun in **Theater II**. The half-cylindrical apex screen at the front of the theater was demolished during the renovation and replaced with a new television-shaped movie screen. . The mirror walls have been removed entirely and replaced with black soundproofing material. The vehicles turn to face the smaller screen to find out the answer to *Final Jeopardy*. Ellen of course wins and defeats Judy. This dry finale can only be described as sad in comparison to the spectacular and all-encompassing effect of the original. The answer to *Final Jeopardy* is "brain power" which ironically wasn't used in crafting the new lackluster finale of the attraction.

The exterior of the pavilion was repainted as part of the 1996 renovation. Pastel colors replaced the black columns and the red-to-yellow radiant energy motif was painted deep blue. The mirrors on the rear flanks of the building were removed and those walls were painted blue as well. The small ponds were filled in at this time and for a period dinosaur topiaries resided inside these new planters for several years. The Brontosaurus topiary which hung its long neck of the queue for the attraction received enough damage from guests hanging from it that Epcot management opted to reroute the queue to the other side of the entrance plaza.

In 2001 the pavilion's sponsor, Exxon, became ExxonMobile and signage within the pavilion was changed. In the post-show area there were also **Save the Tiger Campaign** kiosks installed to support ExxonMobile's conservation endeavor. ExxonMobile failed to renew their sponsorship in 2004 and all references to the company were removed from the show. The dinosaur topiaries were later removed and the pavilion was repainted back to its original color scheme in March of 2009, though the rear walls which previously were covered in mirrors were painted yellow to extend the original color scheme.

Today the attraction remains relatively well received by guests. Of the attractions in Future World though, it is old. Also without a sponsor there is some question as to how much longer the current ride will continue to operate. In terms of the constant cycling that occurs within Future World the Universe of Energy is now the oldest attraction and likely up for replacement if a new sponsor should so choose.

5. WONDERS OF LIFE

TODAY FEW PEOPLE would believe it if you told them the little golden dome fading away in obscurity in Future World East had once been Epcot's most popular attraction. Most guests are blissfully unaware of the dome's existence and the curious few who do happen to notice it poking up from the overgrowth assume it's some sort of backstage facility. An optimistic few even think it might be a new attraction in the process of being built.

Despite Disney's attempts to remove all references to the pavilion – removing all signage, tearing down the DNA helix tower, shutting off the fountains, and silencing the background music – it did exist, and for a period it was the premier attraction at Epcot. Even the most popular modern attractions rarely surge to the five hour waits once seen at **Body Wars** except occasionally on peak holidays. The former Wonders of Life consistently had to control the flow of guests into the building itself at its peak, never mind the extended queues of the individual attractions.

Plans for the **Life & Health** pavilion had been around since Epcot's inception. Disney Legend Frank Armitage joined Imagineering in 1977 and it is said his anatomical artwork paved the way for the **Life & Health** pavilion. A theoretical plan was even presented promotionally in 1978 by Imagineering. This version included a dark ride called **The Incredible Journey Within** that had guests riding through large set pieces of the human body aboard red blood cell vehicles. One spectacular scene included a realistic thirty foot tall beating heart.

Many themes seen in the actualized 1989 Wonders of Life pavilion were already present in the 1978 **Life & Health** pavilion. A circular shaped building contained the central fair-like **Midway of Life** surrounded by the various attractions: the aforementioned dark ride, **Good Health Habits** (a three part animatronic fable), *The Joy of Life* film, and the two shows **Tooth Follies** and **Head Trip**. **Tooth Follies** was a show about the mouth, teeth, and gums. It took place in a theater flanked by pearly white teeth giving the audience the impression they were seated inside the mouth looking out. **Head Trip** was meant to be a humorous tour of the brain with animatronic sprite-like personifications of Emotion, Intellect, and Nervous system. The pavilion changed locations during development, first originating in Future World West in various positions before finally coming into existence between the Universe of Energy and Horizons. The mid-1980s design of the pavilion kept the circus tent theme and combined the various auxiliary shows into a single amalgamation.

1989-2004: The Original

The Wonders of Life was formally announced on June 17, 1987. Ground was broken by February of 1988. The 100,000 square foot pavilion would cost $100 million and grand open to the public on October 18, 1989. Barry Braverman was the show producer on the project. The general layout would consist of four main portions: the main dome, the ride building, the theater building, and the support building bridging the space between the ride and theater. A sloping entrance would wind past a seventy-two foot tall 25-ton spiraling DNA tower sculpture and gushing fountain podiums supporting the entrance archway. The exterior would be revamped slightly during the life of the pavilion – eventually losing the archway when sponsor Metropolitan Life became MetLife – but arriving guests would always enter the dome the same way: on an elevated porch similar in design to the Land pavilion but on a much smaller scale.

Wonders Dome

The 250 foot diameter main dome of the Wonders of Life pavilion held half of the pavilion's show space. The sixty-five foot high domed ceiling had skylights to allow sunlight to stream into the building and allow for an open and airy sensibility amid the turquoise and purple accents of the stark white walls. It had a decidedly 1980s stylized look. A large abstract mobile hung from the center of the dome. Despite the best intentions of the designers the blue and purple glass panels suspended from the free moving arms of the mobile would occasionally collide – resulting in a thunderous clang heard throughout the pavilion. The cast members would take bets on when the collision would next occur.

The main interior portion of the dome with its circulatory walkway was known as the **Fitness Fairgrounds.** The faux-buildings flanking the path were themed as colorful circus tents. On the outer perimeter directly to the left of the main entrance was the **Well and Goods** store. It offered sporting goods merchandise themed to Disney in general. The most popular items were character themed golf clubs and golf balls. To the right of the entrance was the **Pure and Simple** counter service restaurant. Renowned for its Wonder Waffles (Belgian waffles), the location served light and healthy food options compared to most theme park food fare. It included items like salads, pita wraps, fruit & cheese plates, and for reasons unknown: chili cheese dogs.

In the center of the space were three small theaters. To the left of entrance and across from **Well and Goods** was the show *Goofy About Health*. The small theater for *Goofy About Health* included tiered bench seating for approximately 100 guests. It played a clip-montage of Goofy shorts on various screens to illustrate the benefits of healthy living. To the right and across from **Pure and Simple** was the **Anacomical Players** stage with tiered seating similar to *Goofy About Health*. The **Anacomical Players** were a troupe of energetic actors and actresses who did sketch comedy about health, exercise, and nutrition.

The final component of the center of the dome's Fitness Fairground was the **Birth Theater**, home to the film The *Making of Me*. The film was the last portion of the pavilion to formally open on October 30, 1989, with a dedication ceremony on November 2, 1989. The *Making of Me* was a lighthearted sixteen minute film about conception and childbirth starring Martin Short. It was written and directed by Glenn Gordon Caron, produced by Jay Daniel, with music by Bruce Broughton.

The outer ring also included a small attraction called **Coach's Corner**. There guests could enter a batting cage and then receive pre-recorded video feedback on their technique from athletes Gary Carter, Chris Evert, or Nancy Lopez. Additionally there were several **Wondercycles** around the dome which allowed guests to pedal a bike and view a video of simulated travel in synch with the speed of their pedaling. The bikes offered three courses: the shrunken micro course, a trip through Disneyland, and a trip through the Rose Bowl Parade.

Other small attraction areas helped to fill out the outer ring of the Dome. **Frontiers in Medicine** was an exhibit displaying research and achievements in modern medicine. The **MET Lifestyle Review** was a series of consoles that let you input data about yours health and then see a list of recommendations to improve your overall health and well being.

A large area known as the **Sensory Funhouse** explored touch, sight, and sound. It included the **Optical Illusions** tower with multiple spinning and moving visual effects. The **Perplexion Pipes** allowed you to trick your sense of hot and cold by holding a hot pipe and a cold pipe with opposing hands and then holding a normal pipe with both hands which then felt both hot and cold at the same time. A series of headphone shaped booths allowed guests to experience **Audio Antics** by wearing headphones to listen to sound illusions. **Touchy Subjects** offered numerous areas to feel and guess the identity of an object obscured from view. **Reading Brail** lets guests try their hand at reading brail, and last but not least the **Crooked Room** allowed guest climb into a room with distorted perspective.

Body Wars

In 1984 Imagineering was purchasing some interesting new technology, including modified flight training simulators from a company in the U.K. called Redifon. These Advanced Technology Leisure Application Simulators (or ATLAS) were purchased to develop the Star Tours ride with George Lucas for Disneyland. It was decided that if the simulators could convincingly simulate space flight they could also simulate the movement through bodily fluids. **The Incredible Journey Within** became **Body Wars**. This also solved the problem of upkeep and costs related to giant thirty foot beating hearts.

The actual building for **Body Wars** is a separate structure from the main Wonders dome. Guests entering the attraction would approach a series of freestanding arches leading to the edge of the dome. There they would see a large mural on the lower wall of the dome which depicted the interior of the human body. A hidden Mickey could be found in the mural in a cluster of some kind of ganglia that vaguely resembled broccoli. When the attraction first opened the lines would actually extend well beyond this entrance plaza of the ride building. A cast member position called Redirect had to be established who went around the dome changing the Entrance/Exit signs to send guests the proper way around the main circulatory pathway to join the line. This wasn't because the attraction lacked queue space either as the extended queue doubled back along the perimeter of the dome behind **Well and Goods** until it nearly touched the main entrance porch.

The subsequent overflow queue would fill the plaza and archway area with several small switchbacks. **Body Wars** was billed as "The Ride of Your Life!" in print media and was Epcot's first attraction with a height requirement. At the time it opened it was Epcot's ultimate thrill ride.

The story for **Body Wars** was based on the premise that a company called MET was allowing public tours of their **Center for Miniaturization Exploration Technology** along with observation rides in their new body probe vehicles. A number of fictitious characters worked in this center and were introduced to the guests through the public address system and overhead video monitors. The main queue consisted of a long sterile hallway between two pulsing dermatopic purification units, level one and two respectively, which guests had to pass through and be purified by. The combined queue ambiance was contained on laser discs which played the show in a continuous loop.

The public address system would give updates on the status of the four body probe vehicles in service at the various loading bay locations.

BAY 1: Zulu-One-Seven-Four (**Z174**) was ready to load at bay number one, and the spinal dura mater observation team was directed to report to the boarding area. Particle reduction specialist Harris is later requested to bay number one. Finally it was reported that **Z174** had been successfully miniaturized and entered the spinal dura mater. When guests arrived at the loading area **Z174** was listed as departed.

BAY 2: A request was made for the molecular compression specialist to report to bay number two. Shortly afterward, it was reported that body probe Bravo-

Two-Two-Niner (**B229**) had been rolled up to the loading area. The final clearance inspection was reported as now underway. Condition: code yellow. The probe was destined for the epidermal tier to view a splinter. When guests arrive at the loading area **B229** was listed as departing in 5 minutes.

BAY 3: Sierra-Six-Five-Seven (**S657**) was reported as online and ready for miniaturization at bay three. Condition: code green. A request was put out for a Dr. Victoria Humphrey to retrieve an epidermal cell scanner from the bay. Eventually the probe was reported as successfully miniaturized with entry into the occipital-frontalis muscle. Additionally, bay three reported the successful deminiaturization of probe Foxtrot-Eight-One-Seven (**F817**). This probe was not listed on screens as a body probe vehicle and might have been either a mistake or an earlier unmanned probe returning. When guests arrive at the loading area, **S657** was listed as destined for the spongy medulla / tibia with departure 52 minutes later.

BAY 4: This bay only announced final clearance checks for probe Charlie-Two-One-Eight (**C218**) with passenger loading under way at that time. **C218** was the probe guests watch beamed into the Epidermal Tier / Bruise in one of the overhead queue videos. When guests arrive at the loading area **C218** is listed as departed.

MET Alerts would play periodically on the overhead monitors in the queue and present formal addresses to the observation team (guests) from the **MET Center**. The first video, chronologically, introduced Jane – the guest's orientation officer. Jane was a younger woman that many people thought resembled actress Keri Russell. She wore a uniform akin to those of the cast members manning the attraction. The costume can best be described as a grey smock with burgundy trim that looks like something a Star Trek dentist would wear. Jane introduced guests to the twenty-six ton model LGS-250 body probe vehicle. She draws parallels to NASA as she explained the history of MET and how their unmanned probes eventually gave way to manned probes with public observation flights. She also briefly described miniaturization as a "highly sophisticated and ingenious process."

The second video introduced the Mission Control Officer who wore a red commander version of the pseudo-Star Trek uniform. The Control Officer appeared to have no name. He explained how the control tower will observe and ensure the safety of the mission. Eventually he allowed guests to view a vehicle (**C128**) being miniaturized and beamed beneath the skin of a volunteer patient by way of the particle reducer. How exactly a particle reducer worked was not explained.

The final video in the queue introduced the center's chief scientist Dr. Fletcher. While wearing a stylized lab coat the doctor waxed poetically about the advantages of being able to observe the body systems up close and personal. He had a fascination with white blood cells attacking foreign matter like viruses and bacteria. He also emphasized that for safety reasons guests will experience a "routine mission in the sub-skin region" as not to "endanger observers" in the more perilous parts of the human body.

After a few hours or merely the few minutes it takes to walk the length of the queue (depending on if they visited the ride in 1989 or 2004) guests would reach a grouping point where they would be directed to the loading area of the various bays. Despite the entire queue presentation saying probe **B229** was only at bay number two guests could be directed to any of the four bays. The vehicles themselves hold forty passengers in five rows. Rows one, two, and four held eight passengers, while row three held seven and row five held nine.

All four bays would play the same pre-show MET Alert hosted by Mission Control. The Control Officer would introduce your pilot Captain Braddock as he ran pre-flight system checks. Control would also check in with Dr. Cynthia Lair who was floating around inside the volunteer's body and observing the white blood cells attacking a splinter. The mission would be to rendezvous with Dr. Lair and return safely. Captain Braddock was played by Tim Matheson and Dr. Lair by Elisabeth Shue. After the five minute briefing guests would board their **Body Probe** vehicle.

As with many modern attractions, once beamed inside the body something goes horribly wrong. Dr. Lair goes flying off into the body after being hit by a piece of the splinter which broke off just as **B229** arrived on the scene. An epic chase ensued and **B229** flew through many of the body's major systems before it could retrieve Dr. Lair. At that point the batteries were nearly depleted and the team must travel to the brain for an electrical charge. Somehow, defying logic and science, this works and **B229** is able to beam safely back out of the body. The ride was just over five minutes long and was produced by Thomas H. Brodek, from a script written by Scott Hennesy. It was directed by Leonard Nimoy with music by Leonard Rosenman.

Sometime prior to 1992 the ride film was edited to be

about thirty seconds shorter. Notably the **Lung Sequence** was where the most cuts were made. The rhythmic forward and backward lunges of the vehicle as the body volunteer breathed was said to be a primary cause of nausea in early riders. The attraction even featured a sort of triage position just outside the exit of the vehicles to offer guests water and cold compresses should they need the assistance. This position was also responsible for calling over to the load side and reporting any protein spills they discovered so the next set of passengers could be restaged to another loading bay before they entered a soiled vehicle. By all accounts, **Body Wars** was a more thrilling ride than its sister Star Tours.

On May 16, 1995, four-year-old Linda Elaine Baker slumped over in her seat of a **Body Wars** vehicle, unconscious, at approximately three minutes into the ride program. A cast member in the control tower stopped the ride and called for a paramedic. Two nurses aboard the vehicle performed CPR but were unable to revive her. She was pronounced dead after being airlifted to the Orlando Regional Medical Center. An autopsy suggested she likely died of a heart condition known as cardiac conduction defect. There was no evidence that the ride had triggered or exacerbated the condition. Linda's mother reported that she had no health problems at the time, but relatives of the family said she did have a heart ailment. Linda was previously being treated at the University of Texas Medical Branch in Galveston for undisclosed reasons.

Cranium Command

Another building built onto the main dome of the Wonders of Life is the *Cranium Command* theater. It along with Body Wars functions as a covered evacuation location for park guests in the event of an emergency. The dome itself is not rated to withstand the same forces as these auxiliary buildings. Much like **Body Wars**, guests must enter the *Cranium Command* area by first exiting out the side of the dome. A large marquee arch amid the **Sensory Funhouse** area of the dome provided the gateway to the show.

As a culmination of the earlier pavilion show ideas, Cranium was going to star **Captain Cortex**, but eventually the story was adapted to support a rookie brain pilot named **Buzzy**, voiced by Scott Curtis. The primary antagonist of **Buzzy** was to be **General Knowledge** voiced by Corey Burton. Knowledge was the boisterous leader of the brain pilot troops. Guests would watch a short five minute pre-show film that introduced them to **Buzzy** and **General Knowledge** where they learned of **Buzzy's** inexperience as a brain pilot.

Guests would then enter the main *Cranium Command* theater which was designed to resemble the inside of a human head with portals to look out through the eyes as well as screens to communicate with the various bodily functions. As **Buzzy** attempted to manage a day in the life of an adolescent boy he was aided by the **Left Brain** (Charles Grodin), the **Right Brain** (Jon Lovitz), the **Stomach** (George Wendt), the **Bladder** (Jeff Doucette), the **Adrenal Gland** (Bobcat Goldthwait), the **Hypothalamus** (Kirk Wise), and the heart's **Left** and **Right Ventricles** (Dana Carvey, Kevin Nealon). The show was seventeen minutes long and featured **Buzzy** as an animatronic seated in a chair on an arm that could move about the space. All of the other characters appeared in filmed clips on various screens, with the exception of the **Hypothalamus** which was a robot-like creature that rose up from the floor.

2004-2005: Seasonal Status

On June 1, 2001, MetLife ended their sponsorship of the pavilion. As with other pavilions before it, all company references were subsequently removed. **Coach's Corner** was closed and generally abandoned while the rest of the pavilion continued to operate. The **Anacomical Players** were discontinued and their stage left empty.

Problems plagued the rest of the pavilion. As the **Wondercycles** would breakdown they would be carted off backstage and not repaired or replaced. Over time this allowed the **Wondercycle** bike path to be condensed as several fell into disrepair and were removed.

Lack of staffing meant on several occasions The *Making of Me* film simply was not opened to guests. It was considered the least important aspect of the pavilion as far as operations management was concerned. The white triangular insulated panels of the interior dome surface began to occasionally break off and fall down into the dome. Cleaning schedules were deferred and resources directed elsewhere allowing a thick layer of dust to settle atop the awnings of the Fitness Fairgrounds.

Staffing was reduced to bare minimums at **Body Wars** and *Cranium Command*. Attractions that had previously had small armies of workers now operated with one or two cast members. **Body Wars** went from ten or more staff positions during peak periods to just two: one to load the single operating vehicle and one to watch the system in the control tower. A long standing policy to have guests park their strollers out in front of the pavilion was abandoned due to the elimination of the Greeter position at the main dome. Another original function of the Dome Greeter was to watch the capacity of the entire building and to hold guests outside should it near the limit – this was no longer a concern.

On January 4, 2004, the pavilion became listed as a seasonal attraction. It would only operate during peak periods of attendance. **Well and Goods** and **Pure and Simple** both closed entirely. **Frontiers of Medicine** was walled off and the **Wondercycles** were covered over until they were eventually all removed. When the pavilion did open seasonally it often lacked any ambient music and many of the special effects of the **Sensory Funhouse** did not work.

On January 1, 2007, Wonders of Life closed from its final seasonal holiday opening. None of the attractions would open again. Instead the pavilion was repurposed as a special event venue to be used for the annual Flower and Garden Festival and Food and Wine Festival. On August 5, 2007, the exterior DNA helix and the pavilion's marquee were removed. Inside the **Body Wars** mural was painted over, then the lighted signage for the attraction was entirely removed from the wall. The *Making of Me* theater was used to show films on gardening and wine, including the defunct *Seasons of the Vine* film from Disney's California Adventure theme park. The **Sensory Funhouse** was eventually entirely razed to allow for merchandise and sponsor displays. The *Cranium Command* archway was modified to serve as a backdrop for presentations. The entrance and exit of **Body Wars** were walled off. **Pure and Simple's** space would be used as a wine bar and light snack location for various festivals.

Late in 2010 and early 2011 the pavilion was renovated to better suit the twice yearly festivals that would occupy the space. HGTV signed a multi-year contract for the Flower and Garden Festival and subsequently permanent stages were erected within the Dome space. **Coach's Corner**, the remainder of the *Cranium Command* archway, and any vestige of the **Sensory Funhouse** were demolished. Additionally the *Goofy About Health* theater had its interior gutted along with the **Anacomical Players** stage. The two small show venues would become the homes of small stages, while larger stages were erected over area that once were **Coach's Corner** and the entrance plaza to *Cranium Command*. A new mint green and white color scheme was introduced along with polished bronze fixtures and a touch of craftsman architecture in the new design of the space. The pavilion will remain an events venue for the foreseeable future.

6. HORIZONS

ONCE LOCATED in the central position of Future World East, Horizons encompassed all of the themes of Future World and was considered by many to be the heart of Epcot. The phrase "a synthesis of all things Future World" was often used to describe the pavilion. Dramatic advertisements for the new attraction enticed guests to come "take the trip you've always dreamed of."

Few attractions will have the lasting impact that Horizons made on the park going public. Theme parks, and in particular Epcot, run on cycles with rides coming and going as tastes, ideology, and technology changes. Such is the nature of creating the future – but more than ten years after Horizons' demolition fans of the attraction still request its return. First person ride-thru videos and blog posts chronicling its history garner tens of thousands of page views while the original background audio files are traded in prized private collections. Virtual recreations of the ride in its entirety are being actively worked on to this day. Despite this general adoration, Horizons somehow managed to have its critics.

Perhaps the mythology of Horizons makes it out to be something far bigger than it could ever realistically have been. Some modern designers posit that EPCOT Center itself was never actually the altruistic and idealistic endeavor that Horizons portrayed. They suggest it never stood for anything. That it was instead just a theme park – one that successfully leveraged futurism, edutainment, and culture as a marketing scheme. Horizons as we knew it was warm-fuzzy ideology in an elaborate package being sold to consumers. It was nonsensical fluff and for a period guests ate it up. Modern guests are said to be smarter, hipper, and to an extent more cynical about the world around them. It is said they will no longer buy into that sort of mindless idealism.

That sentiment is hard to argue against. If anything it seems to have become the widely accepted viewpoint going forward. Certainly it is reflected in the more modern attractions presented in the park. Horizons' replacement, Mission: SPACE, could easily be considered an emblematic poster child of this change in the design mentality. It could be labeled comparatively just as commercial and crass as Horizons' ever was – not more so – Mission: SPACE is just more transparent about it; a design concession to the enlightened audience.

But maybe that is all wrong. What if the world itself is not so cynical but rather certain powers-that-be have drifted so far from their ideals that they have merely forgotten what it means to stand for something? The fan-made tributes might actually be little eruptions of rebellion against the current status-quo. The core message of Horizons is still true and that is why it continues to resonate with the public. The people now stand for the idea: *If we can dream it, we can do it.*

1983-1999: The Original

When EPCOT Center opened for guests in 1982 the Horizons building was no more than an incomplete partial steel framework. Site prep for the attraction had begun on August 5, 1981, with vertical construction starting January of 1982. The entire project had a twenty-one month construction period. Originally the project was listed as a Phase I pavilion of EPCOT Center, but later became the first of the Phase II pavilions (including Seas and Life/Health) to open.

Back in 1979 Collin Campbell and George McGinnis had developed an **Edison Labs** attraction based on the history of Thomas Edison and his inventions. It would have acted as a gateway to the sponsor, General Electric's, story. This idea was rejected outright by GE's chairman Reginald Jones. He felt a history-filled retrospective had been done already with the company's other sponsored attraction, the **Carousel of Progress**. Jones wanted a show that would feature the future promise of current technology. A show broader in scope based on yesterday, today, and tomorrow began to take shape.

Envisioned as a sequel to the **Carousel of Progress**, the new ride was to feature the same family but a generation older into the future. Tom Fitzgerald was charged with giving warmth and cohesion to the story as various designers roughed out the vignettes. Through the family's ties guests could explore the fantastical world they lived in.

The ride was to be called **Century 3** and reflect America in its third century. As the more broadly cultural aspects of Epcot's World Showcase developed, so did concerns over blatantly basing a Future World pavilion on America and the name was dropped. In 1981 **Futureprobe** became the project's name briefly, but never faired well with GE's executives due to worries about the medical connotation of the word *probe*. Sometime between August and September of 1981 the name of the pavilion became **Horizons**.

George Rester designed the iconic building as it came to exist. Bill Norton, Bob Kurzweil and Claude Coates worked on planning the initial version of the interior. Upon review, Marty Sklar decided the ride should be less film-based and more animatronic-laden. George McGinnis was installed as Project Designer and with his team began to refine the design. He was tasked with eliminating nearly $10,000,000 from the budget. Show scenes were compacted, the pre-show and post-show areas were minimized, and 600 feet of track were eliminated.

The final pavilion would cover three acres. The interior of the two story building would allow for 137,000 square feet of show space. It would require more steel than **Spaceship Earth** to construct - nearly 3,700 tons worth. It rose up seventy-eight feet on the Future World skyline and continued down below ground level to support the massive show scenes. The roof of the building was to be made of five-ply terne-coated steel.

The show scenes would contain thirty human, ten animal, and two robot animatronics. There were more than 770 props and fifty-one special effects spread among the twenty-four major sets. A grand sense of space was to be established with eleven large-scale hand painted backdrops. There were fifteen special effect projections and even after Sklar's request to make the ride less film-based there were still twenty-three film and video projections.

Horizons opened for the Walt Disney World Resort's 12th anniversary on October 1, 1983. The future would never be the same.

Scene 1: Futureport

When approaching Horizons from other Future World pavilions guests were presented with a massive angular gemstone shaped building with a sloping roof and strip of windows looking out into the park. The effect was said to be reminiscent of looking at a spaceship which had just landed in the park. Once inside the pavilion's sliding glass doors the optimistic theme was readily apparent as shining chrome letters on the wall spelled out "*If we can dream it, we can do it.*" The song "New Horizons" could be heard.

> SINGER: Have you ever looked beyond today into the future? Picturing a world we've yet to see. The wonder of finding new ways, that lead to the promise of brighter days.

Down this brief hallway to the right at a T-junction was the departures board of the **Futureport**. It's a bit redundant to say the **Futureport** was futuristic, but the departures listed space shuttles, maglev trains, skylifts, and seatrams as modes of available transportation. The guest's intended destination was a shuttle to Horizons departing from Concourse A, Gate 4, down a path to the left.

For anyone who was curious, Concourse B was implied to be through a pair of stainless steel doors to the right that were installed as part of the overall area design by Gil Keppler. The much-questioned and ever-present trashcan in front of the doors was placed there by Dick Nunis as he decided on trashcan locations during a preview walkthrough of the attraction. The doors were false, did not open, and led nowhere.

Further down the path to the loading area were three kaleidoscopic windows. These created huge spherical illusions by reflecting Bob McCall's concept paintings of Nova Cite, Mesa Verde, and Omega Centauri. Overhead audio played by the windows advertising the destinations. Just beyond these windows was the loading area. The **Futureport** was a small but effective design. The space could hold the entire loaded capacity of the attraction if needed. However practically designed, it did not outpace guest interest, and in the first few years lines for Horizons and its neighbors World of Motion and Universe of Energy often extended back to the Future World East breezeway.

Scene 2: Load

Guests would load by stepping onto a moving walkway running adjacent to the Horizons vehicles. The vehicles and ride system were a new design for Disney. Not quite an omnimover, the ride system traveled in a continuous train sideways, facing outward toward the sets, at approximately 1.5 feet-per-second while suspended from a track above. This unique ride setup was powered by GE-brand motors and drive systems. The ride vehicles themselves were made of Lexan polycarbonate produced by GE.

Every 4.8 seconds another four guests would board one of the 184 vehicles (174 operational, 10 spare). There could be up to 696 guests riding at any given time. With 1,346 feet of track the ride was approximately fifteen minutes long. The subsequent ride narration was beamed into the vehicles via trackside infrared emitters. An announcement informed guests of Horizons 1's departure and declared the ride's destination: The 21st Century, to which the female narrator cut in "That's some destination!"

Scene 3: Transition Tunnel

The ride from this point would be narrated by the elder Husband and Wife pair whose extended family riders would later visit across the globe and in outer space. However, for the first part of the ride they functioned as a sort of running omniscient third-party commentary. There was a humorous duality in their prater. The Husband's voice was the decidedly more serious straight man to the Wife's quips and comic relief. The duo was voiced by Bob Holt and Dena Deitrich.

As innocuous as it may seem, the transition tunnel from the loading area into the ride-proper was no small feat of design and engineering. There were over 177 miles of fiber optic strands utilized in Horizons creating 932,425 end points of light. Of those light points, 21,000 were found in the glowing cloud wall seen in the transition tunnel at the start of the attraction. The lights flashed behind the layers of the sand-blasted acrylic cloud panels to give a soft dreamy effect.

Scene 4: Early Inventions

According to the new hosts, people had been dreaming about the future for centuries and so guests were now invited to take a "look back at tomorrow."

A montage of still images depicting man's early attempts at flight and space travel were presented on an amoeba-shaped screen on the wall in front of the vehicles. These images would wash onto and off of the surface in swirling waves of colored light. The idea was to show that none of the early ideas were terribly practical or particularly safe.

The imagery included a person suspended from a flock of birds and a man suspended from an umbrella with a balloon on top. This would cycle to a "First Moon Flight" captioned image which depicted a stylized group of Victorian on-lookers experiencing a man being shot by giant cannon toward the moon. This was an obvious reference to Jules Verne's book *From the Earth to the Moon*. As the bullet-capsule was shot across the space in its cartoon vignette, the next scene would give riders a glimpse into the interior of the capsule.

Scene 5: Jules Verne

HUSBAND: There's the grand old man himself, Jules Verne. This is the way a moon shot looked to him back in the late 1800s. Old Uncle Jules may not have had all the answers, but he had the right idea.

WIFE: He was just a little ahead of his time.

The Jules Verne scene was the first fully fleshed out and animatronic scene in the attraction. Guests were presented with a life-size recreation of the space capsule as envisioned by Verne. The slick metallic exterior of the capsule gave way to a decidedly Victorian interior which included plush tufted fabric walls for décor and a molded glass sconce. Floating in space along with the man himself was a clucking chicken and companion dog.

Next the vehicle would round a corner and find the capsule's final destination – smack in the face of an anthropomorphic moon. This humorous moon model with its projected face and prop capsule sticking out of its right eye was set amid a field of smiling stars. It was a nod to the 1902 film *Le Voyage dans la Lune* by iconic French film maker Georges Méliès.

Scene 6: Robida Flats

The next scene would take the quirky-French-future motif to the extents of absurdity in a massive cityscape model based on the work of the nineteenth century French futurist Albert Robida. The scene space was filled with two-dimensional flats covered with drawings featuring ideas from the practical to the downright preposterous. Small animations brought the set to life as an endless stream of passengers flooded the subway entrance and women aboard flying-fish drifted up and down in the sky. The Eiffel Tower was busy being constructed in the background.

The black and white flats were enlivened with soft red white and blue lighting representing the French flag. The scene sought to emphasize that people in the past have dreamed up some pretty fantastic views of the future.

WIFE: And some pretty mixed up ones, too.

Scene 7: Art Deco / Easy Living

A shared background painting behind the right edge of the Robida Flats scene would become the fantastical vista beyond a wall of windows in a posh art deco living space. The background painting, with its sphere-topped and conical building towers, was based on the illustration called *City of the Future* by Frank R. Paul. The illustration was originally created for the back cover of the April 1942 *Amazing Stories* magazine. Notably, the Horizons version of the image seems to be based on the September 1996 reprint in the magazine *Fantastic Stories* which crops out much of the lower portion of the image.

The large animatronic filled art deco scene was commonly called Easy Living due to the narration touting: "Easy living, it's always just around the corner." There guests would see what could be considered a typical 1920s or 1930s sci-fi home of the future.

A man in a smoking jacket peered out the aforementioned windows as his robot butler vacuumed the floor. On a second level platform a woman is bathing in a bubble bath. All of her naughtier bits are hidden from view as she watches a giant deco-styled television showing a man singing "There's a Great Big Beautiful Tomorrow" the theme song from GE's **Carousel of Progress** attraction. In truth, this female character was actually fairly realistically sculpted, entirely nude, and only had one leg. This was presumably done entirely for the amusement of imagineers working on the project. Guests would never be able to see anything below her shoulders as they were looking upward at her from a steep angle from the passing vehicles.

Down below the opulent bubble bath was another man who was seated in a well-equipped chair of the future. One robot cuts his hair while another tans his skin and the chair itself works on his shoe shine. The Tan-O-Matic offered several levels of tanning to indulge the man: Hawaiian, Caribbean, Miami Beach, or Palm Springs. A nearby device from the Atmospheric Storage Company blows either Tropical Breezes or Alpine Chill to regulate the temperature.

The final vignette of the art deco apartment was a robot chef wildly destroying the kitchen with its multiple arms. Dishes and partially baked goods were everywhere as the robot's head spun around and around. One arm cooked, one arm attempted the dishes, another swept the floor, all while a final hand was seen pouring milk into an overflowing dish on the ground. A small white cat eagerly lapped the milk up off the floor. This cat was reportedly a hotly desired keepsake once the attraction closed.

Scene 8: Neon City Screens

According to the narrators, guests were now "just in time for the matinee." The scenery transitioned into a series of three screens surrounded by neon theatrical marquees. The first screen played *Metropolis* (Fritz Lang, 1926), *Modern Times* (Charlie Chaplin, 1936), and *Woman in the Moon* (Fritz Lang, 1928). They presented a brief history of science fiction from the 1920s with an emphasis on industrial imagery, whimsy, and the common man. The second screen played *Just Imagine* (David Butler, 1930), *Things to Come* (William C. Menzies, 1936), and *Buck Rogers* (Ford Beebe & Saul A. Goodkind, 1939), delving into the 1930s with a dramatic score and flying sequences.

The finale screen was shaped like a television and played the 1958 *Disneyland* television show episode entitled *Magic Highway USA*. It depicted the family car of the future and how it will be washed, fueled, and driven automatically.

Scene 9: Negative Space

Scene numbers for the chronology of Horizons being used for this book are based off the audio department's recordings and subsequently there are points where no discernable scene or audio listing is apparent. For all intents and purposes Scene 9 appears to just be a black wall that links the prior and forthcoming scenes. Designers at WDI are known to refer to this as intentional negative space which allows for dramatic juxtaposition of scenic elements to "nothingness" for the most dramatic effect. If every scene was full and continuous into one another the theory goes that it would all become indiscernible noise. So negative space in attractions functions much the same way as a scene fades in film or a blackout occurs in theater – it allows there to be a cognitive break between parts.

In this book it's allowing us to answer a fairly common question that arose in the minds of many riders right about this time in their journey. Where does one go if the ride stops or breaks down?

The vehicles continuously traveled sideways and were entered from a pair of small sliding door panels at the front. There's nothing but massive show sets in front of the vehicles once they depart the load station and several of these scenes have a considerable drop-off down into vast amounts of open space. In the Omnimax and Space scenes the vehicles would be suspended a full sixty-five feet above the ground level. To remedy this issue the vehicles had escape hatches on the backside that could be opened by cast members as needed. These hatches allowed guests to unload onto a hidden walkway which ran behind the entire length of the vehicle path.

Regardless, only a select minority of guests would ever be in a vehicle facing one of the blank walls in the attraction when the ride broke down – left to ponder such things in detail – as the ride reportedly broke down infrequently.

Scene 10: Future City

The brief moment of palette cleansing darkness and silence would give way to a cacophony of sights and sounds in the Future City scene. This large diorama depicted the future from the 1950s in a full blacklight painted neon glory. Akin to the Robida Flats in scope and presentation, the Future City took the concept one step further with honking traffic horns and bright neon colors. Rocket packs shot across the sky and the highways of the future were jammed with little Jetson-like cars. A neon DNA-helix morphed into high-rise condos of the future.

Early plans for the ride called for 1950s scene to actually be art deco with animatronic characters. This was scaled down as the design process progressed. In one of the later design changes, John Hench noted that the design team was not using the full height of the available space. He inserted a rocket tower resembling the Seattle Space Needle. This tower went against the original attempt to lower the budget of the scene, but was so liked by the other designers for creating a center of interest in the scene that it stayed.

Scene 11: Omnimax Entry Tunnel

"A darkened tunnel with ambient synthesizer music of an even and decidedly solemn pace accented with the crashing waves synthesizer motif found in many areas of EPCOT Center."

The entry tunnel to the Omnimax theater is more notable for what it wasn't rather than what it was. Strips of red and pink lights along the top of the dark wall alternated to create a gentle but active glowing effect. Originally this was further accented by thousands of fiber optic light points. For some reason in the life of the attraction this effect was removed and only the alternating top lights remained. The whole scene was meant to emphasize the return from the past to the present, sort of a bookend compliment to the initial entry tunnel with its fiber optics.

> **WIFE:** I suppose people have always dreamed of the future. We sure do.

> **HUSBAND:** The only difference is that today, with what we know and what we're learning to do, we really can bring our dreams to life. It takes a lot of work, but the truth is, if we can dream it, we can do it.

This portion of the ride was extensively redesigned from the original Claude Coates concept to save some budget. In that version the vehicles rose along a spiral track to enter the Omnimax theater at the top level, rather than sloping upward through the 1950s scene and Omnimax entry tunnel as it did in the final design. Along the spiral turns guests would have seen a montage of *Amazing Stories* cover artwork and a continuation of future concept projections seen earlier in the ride. As it came to exist, for the majority of riders it was a quiet and unassuming darkened tunnel with an optimistic message in the narration.

WIFE: Tomorrow's Horizons are here, today!

Scene 12: Omnimax Theater

With a grand musical crescendo the darkened tunnel would give way to a massive 80' x 120' projection space. The two hemispherical Omnimax projections screens were so large that they had to be built in place while the ride building itself was still just a shell. The music by George Wilkins would build to a rousing climax as scenes showed the possibilities of the future people were building "today." The score was accented heavily with a synthesizer played by Michael Boddicker and pipe organ played by Richard Bolks to achieve the proper grand effect.

Scenes projected in the Omnimax sequence included computer imagery of DNA, the sun and solar energy, the space shuttle taking off and then docking with a space station, Landsat photography, the New York City skyline, a close-up of a computer chip with silicon processor which morphs into growing crystal structures, and finally ocean exploration. This would then loop back to the DNA sequence. Each scene transitioned dramatically to the next, for example the DNA would unravel and swirl to become the sun before the sun would fade away into the horizon as the space shuttle's rockets ignited. The booming sound of the space shuttle launch was amplified by subwoofers positioned in the base of the vehicle seats.

Originally the Omnimax theaters were planned as not just two screens, but rather a three-screen triple Omnimax experience. When the third screen was discarded to lower the budget, so were several image concepts for the extended video loop. Among them were imagery of weather systems including a bird's eye view of flying through a hurricane, astronauts training in water tanks, images of a cityscape and the human body in infrared thermal relief, the VLA collection of radio telescopes, laser surgery, and even robot manufacturing. The water tank training would later reappear inside Mission: SPACE and the robot manufacturing would later gain prominence at Test Track.

Designer George McGinnis has remarked that on an initial ride-through of the attraction with Dick Nunis, then head of Disney Parks & Resorts, that Nunis said he would have liked the ride vehicles to have simulator movements synchronized to the projections. It was far too late in the design process for that sort of change, but the idea would eventually be realized in the subsequent Soarin' attraction.

Scene 13: Omnimax Exit Tunnel

The Omnimax exit tunnel was a mirror image of the entry tunnel in both audio and visual. It too originally had forty miles of fiber optic and 22,000 points of lights.

> **HUSBAND:** What you've just seen are the building blocks for the future up ahead. And while it may look fantastic, remember, it's all possible.

> **WIFE:** That's right.

HUSBAND: And we ought to know, we live there. Come on, take a look at 21st century living: on land, at sea, and even out in space. But let's start off at our place.

Scene 14: Urban Habitat

The 21st century Urban Habitat, otherwise known as Nova Cite, was home to our narrators. Here guests finally saw the narrators in animatronic form: the Husband at the Aeolian harp synthesizer, which he played poorly to the dismay of their dog while the Wife was on the couch talking to her daughter via holographic phone. The Urban Habitat was the start of the section of the ride often referred to as Tomorrow's Windows where guests would see options of future living in the 21st century.

Outside the large window panels of the apartment was a vast angular cityscape with numerous maglev trains zipping past. It was an optimistic version of city growth with lots of green landscaping. It even had tennis courts and a swimming pool amid the angular buildings of the scenic background. Inside the apartment itself the low wrap-around sectional seating and dozens of small colorful pillows in the room can best be described as a futuristic version of modern Scandinavian design – as if they shopped at the Space IKEA.

There were small nods to other areas of the attraction yet to be visited like the visages of the entire daughter's family in Mesa Verde. A photograph of the actress who plays their red-haired grand daughter was in a picture frame on low shelf near an acrylic candle holder. There was also a photograph of the couple's Captain Nemo look-alike son-in-law on a shelf near the dining room table.

Most noticeable was the holographic phone in the middle of the living space. The phone worked, in functional real world terms, by reflecting a small puppet of the daughter in Mesa Verde in front of a background which resembled the forthcoming Mesa Verde harvester scene. The whole puppet and background setup was physically located above the ride vehicles. The staircase behind the Husband led to the catwalk above the ride path where the puppet resided.

As the vehicles rounded the scene and began to exit they were brought past a large array of fanciful fruit and vegetables. Designer Alex Taylor was the one who dreamed up the new plants seen on the Nova Cite balcony. *Circuit Egg Ivy* grew in a kinked and twisted pattern resembling an electronic circuit from sconces on the walls. *Flavor Grapes* grew in clusters of different colors and flavors. *Pinanas* were a combination of pineapples and bananas while *Loranges* were meant to be a lime/orange hybrid. One mysterious plant resembling a sea anemone and bird of paradise hybrid was found in a vase on the kitchen table and has never been identified. It is thought to be a possible nod to the Sea Castle scenes ahead.

Scene 15: Mesa Verde Transition

As with Scene 9, it appears that Scene 15 never really existed. However, it was the point in the ride where the vehicles began their descent downward to the lower level of the building.

Scene 16: Desert Farm

The desert farm scene of Mesa Verde has the daughter in full animatronic form in Control Station 4 growing the aforementioned theoretical fruits on a farm made out of a terraformed desert landscape. Specifically she and a fleet of robot hover-ships were growing and tending to loranges. Loranges were genetically modified to grow towards the outside of the trees to make it easier for the robots to harvest. In her control room the daughter had samples of pinanas, loranges, and flavor grapes with various genetic combinations. They were based on ideas from the consultation of Carl Hodges, director of the Environmental Research Lab at the University of Arizona. The daughter was attempting to finish the harvest before an approaching storm which her husband, a Captain Nemo look-alike, calls to tell her about on a video phone.

The entire scene smelled like oranges thanks to Disney's smellitizer technology and the Flavor and the Fragrance Specialties Company's industrial scent division called Flavorscents. The scent used for the scene was Orange Scent Fragrance #71383.

Geographically speaking, Mesa Verde was part of the Sonoran Desert. The voice controlled robotic harvesters lifted baskets of crops in front of a large forced perspective backdrop. The perspective effect of the background only worked properly when viewed in the middle of the scene. Gil Keppler and George McGinnis detailed the desert farming scene and had to come up with ways to counteract the problem. The harvesters' odd shape was designed to never be out of perspective. The control room itself was round in shape and thereby created a foreground element that always looked correct in perspective. The Pegasus hoverlift on the pad next to the control room distracted riders from the background which at that viewing angle would be dramatically out of perspective. The hoverlift itself had turbine-like blades in its wings to create lift that were weathered with red dust akin to the Mesa Verde surroundings. Keen eyes could even spot road-runners in the desert landscape.

Scene 17: Desert Habitat Kitchen

The vehicles rounded a rocky corner to enter the home of the desert family. The rockwork had a waterfall effect that created a small stream that continues through the scene – past the tri-apple tree and a little cat drinking water from the pool until it flowed under the home. The tri-apples weren't three times as big, just three times the apple in one as if they were stacked on top of each other. The water feature continued underneath the elevated, circular, and glass-bottomed kitchen of the home which revealed the craggy rocks and cactus of Mesa Verde's natural landscape.

The farmer's husband and son were found in the kitchen. The husband prepared a birthday cake topped with a Brava Centauri model and wrapped presents at a center console. Her son, Michael, teases his father and the voice activated refrigerator as it constantly opens and closes to try and provide him with the various food items he requests. General Electric advised on the various electronics found in the kitchen. In addition to the voice activated fridge there was a Laser Chef oven and clear food domes built into the counter. Built into the upper-cabinets the Laser Chef, one of two, was busy cooking a turkey at 350° F. The kitchen computer monitor, which was presumably the video phone for the husband to talk to his wife, was actually a light hidden in the set.

The visage of the Nemo look-alike husband was that of Pete Renoudet who is best known as the voice of Henry and Max from the Country Bear Jamboree as well as narration for the defunct Twenty Thousand Leagues Under the Sea ride at the Magic Kingdom. The use of his face was last minute change in the ride's development and the animatronic had to be hastily re-skinned. Mr. Renoudet's voice, however, was not used as designers kept the original actor's audio and had Pete lip-synch the video phone segments.

Scene 18: Communications Room

A few steps down from the kitchen to the right was the family's living room or communications room. Natural rockwork of the surrounding landscape was integrated into this second circular structure. There was a random gazelle statue at the base of the steps down from the kitchen, just below a pair of tiered hanging pendants filled with plants on a clear acrylic column. In this space an animatronic of the red-haired daughter (granddaughter of the narrators) spoke to her boyfriend on a large video screen built into the rear wall of the room.

The room's décor mostly consisted of pastel paneled walls and some potted cacti. Built into a smaller wall unit near the granddaughter was the fictional Athene Series 2500 personal computer featuring a 4 by 5 inch screen and built-in backlit QWERTY keyboard. It ran on discs, one of which was labeled "Micro Video Disk Pack, Advanced Chemistry Unit 4." For a bit of kitsch there was an obsidian obelisk and a jade creature resembling some sort of lion atop the computer system. On shelves nearby there were "MA-2 Discs" in large boxes grouped alphabetically containing "Films/Programs" and family videos in slimmer disc boxes.

HUSBAND: Shouldn't your granddaughter be studying instead of flirting with that beach boy?

On the big screen was designer Tom Fitzgerald portraying the love interest of the red-haired daughter. Though his name isn't mentioned in the scene, designers have referred to this character as Tom II. He is seen working on his SoloSub at Sea Castle and speaking in an endless loop about how he is never late.

WIFE: He is not a beach boy! He's studying marine biology there on the floating city.

Scene 19: Sub Repair Room

The view suddenly switched to Tom II's side of the conversation at Sea Castle and the granddaughter was portrayed on a large screen with her half of the conversation. This film loop is a bit more informative than the last – the daughter was goading him not to be late for the party and he needs to not miss the Sunset Express maglev to the desert, as he had already missed the flyer. Actress Corinne Cook played the daughter in this particular video sequence.

The sub repair room was a tall three level scene where the ride vehicles travel downward toward the base of the show building. The top portion had the formal sub repair room with Tom II animatronic working on his SoloSub. Underneath that was a level with another SoloSub that extended to the right to reveal the Undersea Classroom. At the lowest level was an opening to the water with yet another SoloSub sitting on the ocean floor.

Through the windows of the upper level riders could see a portion of the floating city. Shim Yokoyama created this large sea-level perspective painting at the request of George McGinnis after Bob Kurzweil had previously rendered the floating city from a high viewpoint. The painting featured a sleek multi-level modern resort. The bulk of the tiered and sloped building (akin to the Contemporary Resort) was held above the water level by large streamline moderne columns that extended above and below the main building. They were shaped reminiscent of ocean liner smokestacks. Pendants-shaped portions hung from the mid-level and create what appear to be large observation decks just above the water. The whole resort building appeared to be c-shaped, creating an artificial cove, with the rider's vantage point looking out from the center to see the sides curving in on the horizon. The surrounding landscape was dotted with tropical palms. The water surface all around the structure had sea craft docked, including numerous SoloSubs. There was a similarly styled barrier island with buildings visible in the distance, adding a sense of depth to the scene.

Scene 21: Undersea Classroom

Down on the second level and to right of the sub repair room was the Undersea Classroom. A group of children and their teacher prepared for an educational dive along with a trained seal named Rover. The classroom itself was a circular room with a grated floor that was flanked with bench seating and prominently featured a large television toward the rear. The television listed the classroom schedule: "9:30 Sr. Lifesaving, 10:00 Discovery Dive, 11:30 Swim Team Practice, 13:00 SoloSub race, 14:00 Jr.

Lifesaving." Designer George McGinnis' children Shana and Scott posed as models for two of the animatronics in the undersea classroom. Scott was the boy playing with the seal while Shana was the little blond girl tapping her toes.

Scene 22: Undersea Resort

The vehicles would round a sharp corner and double back almost facing 180 degrees back toward where they had just been. Through an ingenious bit of design the Undersea Classroom and the Undersea Resort scenes were compacted as a single thin set piece with two audience-facing sides. Essentially the Undersea Resort's restaurant is built out of the rear wall of the classroom with maintenance access through the scene itself. If guests looked behind the various columns of the classroom scene they could see into the restaurant booths.

The scene was a series of acrylic hemispheres poking out from what was supposed to be the lower submerged levels of the Sea Castle resort. An architectural structure would wrap around the vehicle path to give the illusion of traveling through an underwater tunnel with windows looking out into the ocean. The entire exterior of Sea Castle had a diamond panel texture. Large pieces of fake kelp were hung from floor to ceiling

In the first bubble of the restaurant there is a black couple eating shrimp cocktail, and wearing what one might call 1970s African style head wraps in bright orange patterns. The man's face was the same sculptural face used for the banjo player in World of Motion and the American Adventure. Each of the bubble windows had an outside rail – perhaps as theoretical bumpers to protect the clear hemispheres from passing submarines. On a practical level the bar allowed the seal to float to look at the little Asian girl in the second bubble. The girl leans far out into the bubble to see the seal. She and her mother wore traditional Asian garb, including mandarin collars and cap sleeves with a bit of 1970s retro styling thrown in for good measure. Her mother is holding a lovely silk purse with a beaded strap and shows a complete disregard for a guardrail that should be keeping her daughter out of the bubble itself.

The third window of the restaurant was a bit more futuristic than the others. A single man sits at the table looking over a menu. The menu could be thought of as sort of like the modern Apple iPad. It had buttons which were connected to printed circuitry on the otherwise clear panel. The text appeared to be lorum ipsum, or fake Latin commonly used by writers and artists just to fill in space. There was also a picture of a lobster, so it was presumably some sort of seafood restaurant. Notably the color and details of the whole scene were reminiscent of the forthcoming Sea Base Alpha design for the Living Seas (which opened three years after Horizons).

Scene 23: Undersea Industry

Leaving the resort structure behind, the vehicles would venture out into the open ocean. A rear-projection screen showed the earlier diving class beginning their dive. Their destination was the nearby kelp farm.

> **HUSBAND:** There's always been something sort of mysterious about our oceans. We knew they were filled with valuable gifts for us.

WIFE: Yeah, water and seaweed.

HUSBAND: Very funny. But seawater has become an excellent source of energy as well as being valuable for desert irrigation. And kelp…

WIFE: Seaweed.

HUSBAND: Kelp is a tremendous source of low cost fuel. Oh, we've found lots of good things under our oceans.

Dimly lit vignettes depicted the deep ocean with bustling machinery harvesting kelp and other goods. An octopus sat atop a nearby rock and blinked at the passing vehicles as a large robotic arm scoured the sea floor.

Scene 24: Sea/Space Transition

WIFE: And don't forget space! We've found lots of good things out there, too.

Scene 24 is another non-existent scene but for this instance there was very much an intent to have an actualized scene in the space. The SoloSub and Intercolony Shuttle were designed to look alike. A special effect was attempted where one morphed to the other as guests entered outer space from the undersea darkness. The attempted effect was to be done with projections as designed by Don Iwerks. When it was built in place in the attraction it didn't work properly. The projection chassis vibrated too much because of the ride system. It was removed prior to opening and never replaced.

Scene 25: Outer Space

A very fluid transition would occur as the ride vehicles would begin to rise up higher into the show building from the darkness of the sea to the star fields of open space. For many guests the most memorable portion of Richard Bellis' attraction score would play at this point, simply entitled "Space." At the apex of the space-entry climb the vehicles were again sixty-five feet in the air.

Floating in space was an astronaut attempting to attach pieces of truss together with guidance from his female captain in a small robotic-armed vehicle. They were building a new rotating space colony, Omega Centauri. In the distance guests could see the projection of a completed rotating space colony, Brava Centauri.

The model built for the rotating space colony projection film was constructed as an eight foot sphere. Inside it had over 8,000 miniature lights to accent the internal landscape which was visible as it rotated. The same model was also used for the forthcoming Choose Your Tomorrow Simulation sequence.

Scene 26: Space Colony

Passing a Century III Intercolony Shuttle parked in Bay 37 riders would formally enter into the Brava Centauri space station. In the center column a series of large windows allowed guests to look toward the interior of the rotating colony and see Shim Yokoyama's elaborate painted background of the habitats, homes, stadiums and parks within the colony.

Careful observers could make out Space Mountain and Disneyland's Main Street USA in the image. Designers worked with Princeton physicist Gerard O'Neill to hash out the realistic and practical details of the entire space colony. The narrators commented the space colony was the home of their son and his family.

Scene 27: Health and Recreation

At the whim of the narrators guests would then explore the space colony, beginning with a zero-gravity gym. Visible activities included a woman pedaling a stationary bicycle upside-down in front of a domed projection of an Earth road.

There was also an unoccupied rowing machine set up similarly as the stationary bike, with options for the accompanying scenery of Louisiana Bayou, Colorado River, or Venice Canals. The silhouette of a space basketball game occurring in another room was visible. Further, an automated health scan machine was visible in the main room.

Scene 28: Main Shuttle Port

Next was another shuttle port area where a new family was arriving at the space colony and trying to get their bearings. The father attempted to retrieve his son's lost magnetic shoe much to the bemusement of the mother. The dog (Napoleon) and son (Timmy) floated around excitedly in the space.

A nearby panel indicated the shuttle the family has arrived on was named the Santa Maria. Greg Wilzbach was responsible for detailing this particular scene. George McGinnis' son Reed served as the model for Timmy.

Scene 29: Crystal Lab

Next door was a laboratory where a female scientist was growing a crystal at the end of a robotic arm in the middle of the space. The scientist floated freely and the controls for the lab's Defractometer A and B were mirrored to allow for multi-angle zero-G operations. Designers consulted with NASA and Cal Tech's Jet Propulsion Lab on the prospect of growing crystals for semiconductors in space. The team generally believed the size of the crystal presented was far too massive, but it was allowed to stay under the mantra of "if you can dream it."

Scene 30: Transition

WIFE: Uh, oh. We got to run.

HUSBAND: Time for our grandson's party?

WIFE: Uh, huh.

HUSBAND: We'll catch up to you later.

Scene 31: Holographic Party Line

The last room of the space colony is the home of the narrators' son, his wife, and their grandson Davey. A birthday party had been arranged with the various family members calling in on holographic phone lines. The phone parties make up a series of panels above the family reclining on a couch near a UFO-themed birthday cake. The use of the pepper's ghost effect creates the various holographic images. From left to right is the narrator duo, the red-haired granddaughter from Mesa Verde holding the cake prepared by her brother and father, and finally Tom II – who apparently was in fact late and had to call in on his own. Together they sing Happy Birthday to Davey.

Scene 32: Options Models

As the vehicles drifted away from this quiet birthday party scene an announcement would play indicating that Horizons 1 was ready for final boarding. A series of window advertisements were presented: Omega Centauri – Now Open, Mesa Verde, and Sea Castle Resort. Small models of the Intercolony Shuttle, Pegasus Hoverlift, and SoloSub were behind concave glass giving the impression of their movement across the space as the vehicles passed.

This began what was called the Countdown Sequence. Alarms chimed and various alerts flashed on panels in the walls in front of the vehicles. "Launch Sequence Initiated," "Systems Check Complete," "Air Lock Open," and "Launch" flashed on and off.

Scene 33: Choose Your Tomorrow Select

The vehicles drifted into a star field as an announcement came on overhead.

FEMALE ANNOUNCER: Attention Horizons passengers. You are invited to choose your own flight path back to the Futureport. Please look down at the lighted panels in front of you. Press one of the three ride choices: Space, Desert, or Under Sea. Everyone can choose, majority rules. All passengers make your selections now.

Panels in the front of the vehicles would suddenly light up offering three choices: Space, Desert, or Under Sea. As mentioned in the announcement, the most popular choice in a vehicle would win. Divider panels between the vehicles would deploy at this point, acting as blinders, preventing the vehicles from seeing each other's upcoming presentations. Originally this sequence was planned as a video recap of the ride instead of the star tunnel before guest chose their ending.

Scene 34: Choose Your Tomorrow Simulation

Depending on the rider's choice one of three films would play on a long screen in front of the vehicles as they continued their sideways motion. The film would simulate the journey back to the Futureport by flying through space, the ocean, or over the desert landscape. Seven of GE's Talaria light-valve projectors were utilized for the finale movie sequence. These projectors moved on their own track in-synch with the vehicles. Engineer Marty Kindle worked out the logistics that would enable each car to see a different environment. Each vehicle would tilt ten degrees backwards and utilize low-frequency transducers in the vehicle to create the feeling of acceleration through space.

The films were developed by Marty Kindle. They had different visuals but the same implied motions and timings. The models for the films were constructed under the guidance of David Jones. The project took two years of designing, constructing, and filming. The desert film was the longest continuous sequence ever filmed with miniatures. The models for the finale films measured eighty-two feet across. The desert model was built in a hangar at the Burbank airport and the space model in

Disney's own Stage 3. The underwater model had two parts. One was shot and then swapped for the other half. The sequence was shot dry with smoke added to produce the underwater haze effect.

Each sequence took thirty minutes to shoot. A computer was used to get a precise camera path and a special gantry system was constructed to keep the camera from casting a shadow over the model. The films were only thirty-one seconds long.

Initially there were four choices. A maglev flight through downtown Nova Cite was also planned but discarded due to budget constraints.

Scene 35: Tunnel to Unload

The originally planned ending of the attraction was going to be the Omnimax sequence. When the Omnimax scene moved to the middle of the ride it left the ride briefly without an ending until the Choose Your Tomorrow sequence was designed. The ride's exit area was originally a series of speedramps in tubes with projections of GE imagery. The images would track guests as they moved along the speedramps. Jack Welch, chairman of GE, thought it was too commercial for a post-show. The idea morphed into the choose your ending sequence.

Scene 36: Unload

When originally opened the exit area featured a huge mural by Bob McCall. The 19' x 60' painting was called *The Prologue and the Promise*. It was based on other concept art created for Horizons. The exit mural was subsequently removed after GE became concerned with exit polls which stated most guests could not identify the ride's sponsor. A glowing GE-themed corridor was added to give a lasting impression of the pavilions sponsor.

In 1993 the sponsorship contract with General Electric was winding down. Wren Aber, Horizons' manager of corporate operations, commented that plans were being considered for a Space-themed pavilion but that a Space pavilion would be expensive and GE might not be a part of it. Any future pavilion GE was involved in, Aber said would need to be greatly updated and upgraded.

September 30, 1993, General Electric stopped sponsoring the pavilion. Horizons continued to operate with all signs of GE removed until late 1994 when it closed and formally became a seasonal attraction. The ride reopened in December 1995 due to concerns over the park capacity as World of Motion closed to change into Test Track and the Universe of Energy closed to convert to Ellen's Energy Adventure. During this period major problems with roof leaks became obvious in the space colony scenes and the general condition of the overall experience deteriorated dramatically.

A major rehabilitation of the attraction was considered. Improvements would have included new Omnimax films, new sets for the futuristic scenes, updated projection technology, new animatronics, updated wardrobes, and a new musical score. With no sponsor Michael Eisner decided it was too expensive. Finally the pavilion closed January 9, 1999. It would later be demolished entirely and replaced with Mission: SPACE in a new building on the site.

7. MISSION: SPACE

THE JOURNEYS IN SPACE pavilion was considered for Epcot as early as 1978. The earliest versions of the attraction proposed a huge show building housing an orbiting space station design. The theoretical building would look like a launch pad with a spacecraft ready for takeoff. After an omnimover ride through space and into orbit guests would have a choice of several hands-on exhibit areas or entering a main show presentation. This simulation, designed with the assistance of Ray Bradbury, would have had vast walls of windows gazing out into space and down to earth. Think **Mission to Mars** on steroids. With its spectacular rotating gravity walls it was to be the centerpiece of the **Journeys in Space** pavilion. This massive undertaking was shelved without a sponsor. It was later resubmitted after 1982 when Epcot's second group of pavilions was being considered. Phase II attraction **Living Seas** took the original **Journeys in Space** plot, pushing the pavilion's new theoretical location over between Seas and Land. This location remains a viable expansion pad in Future World for a large attraction to this day.

In 1990 **Journeys in Space** was proposed again with a redesign in the physical environments. Delta was considered a possible sponsor, but the project stalled due to a lack of financing. After GE left **Horizons** in 1993 the shell of the **Horizons** show building was thought suitable for a third space pavilion design. The entire pavilion would be gutted allowing guests to enter the now hollow and expansive show building to be filled with interactive guest space and hands on activities. It would have utilized the full height of the Omnimax screens without the **Horizons** ride system to provide a star field backdrop. A small portion of the **Horizons** ride track was to be preserved for a new ride – a suspended spacewalk experience.

Computer company Compaq entered talks for a Space-themed pavilion in 1999. The talks primarily focused on a pre-show element from one of the many **Journeys in Space** designs: an enhanced G-force simulation. On April 20, 2000, **Mission: SPACE** was announced to the world as a coming Epcot attraction.

After demolishing **Horizons**, work on the site began for the new pavilion and by late 2000 the foundations were poured and vertical construction was set to begin. By the summer of 2001 a preview display opened in **Innoventions East** promoting the attraction. A small setback occurred in September 2001 as Compaq and Hewitt Packard announced a merger. The prevailing brand, HP, would be the featured sponsor of the attraction and the pavilion's signage was redesigned. Three-and-a-half years after research and design had started one bay was ready for test and adjust by September 2002. The pavilion would be completed and handed over to Epcot operations on May 30, 2003, with previews beginning the week after. The **Mission: SPACE** pavilion was formally dedicated October 9, 2003.

2003-2006: The Original

At its core the experience of the intended space pavilion had changed from being a "space journey" into a "space flight training" experience – thereby avoiding the complexities of establishing a semi-plausible back-story for getting guests to outer space and back. Guests enter the fictional **International Space Training Center** (ISTC) in the year 2036 to be recruited and trained as space pioneers. The storyline makes it clear that guests are never to actually leave planet earth during their training exercise.

The ISTC's curvilinear building is fronted by the **Planetary Plaza**. Three large celestial bodies are depicted in sculptural form in the plaza. The largest, Jupiter, is sixteen feet in diameter, while Earth is the smallest at a mere ten feet. The Earth sculpture sits on a pedestal and rotates while being wrapped by the swirling **Mission: SPACE** marquee. The nearby Moon sculpture is twelve feet in diameter and covered in markers showcasing the various historic manned and unmanned missions to the lunar surface. The walls of the plaza have plaques with quotes by famed space explorers and supporters of space exploration.

Guests enter into the building through a large red sphere on the front of the building meant to resemble Mars. The storyline of the attraction is based around the training of guests explicitly for the future colonization of Mars. Over a hundred shades of red were considered in finding the exact tone for the spherical entryway. Inside the 45,000 square foot ride building guests zigzag past models of futuristic spacecraft and a thirty-five foot tall gravity wheel. At the end of the queue guests are sent into a **Briefing Room** in groups of four up to a total of ten groups or forty astronaut trainees per ride bay. There are four pre-show areas and ride bays, originally denoted in color as red, blue, green, and yellow.

The **Pre-Show** spaces feature overhead televisions that play an introduction to space training led by CapCom played by Gary Sinise. Multiple warnings are played about the intensity of the attraction and the ability to opt-out of the experience by alerting a uniformed crew member. Many guests have remarked that the constant warnings are more frightening the actual attraction. The pre-show also introduces guests to the fictional X-2 spacecraft that will be propelling them into space in their training.

After the pre-show guests are moved into a circular **Pre-Boarding Hallway** surrounding the ride bay of the attraction. The ten groups are spaced evenly around the bay in this hallway with each passenger standing atop a number on the floor in front of an entry door to the ride bay. Next to the entry door a screen plays a second pre-show video sequence featuring CapCom and more warnings about the intensity of the attraction. The pre-show also highlights each of the four passengers-per-pod's designated jobs during the simulated mission to Mars: Pilot, Engineer, Commander, or Navigator. It is explained that pushing button on the console within the pod will activate their various duties during the ride.

One final warning later, the doors to one of the four

Ride Bays opens and guests enter their **Ride Capsule**. An over-the-shoulder harness secures each rider in their seat and the entire capsule closes like a clamshell. Individual video screens are mere inches in front of each rider's face. To lower the chances of nausea a cooling breeze blows on rider's races from an air conditioning system.

Each of the centrifuges for the ride system is anchored in a basement thirty feet below ground where the ride motor is also situated. The space training flight includes scenes of the shuttle launch, a slingshot around the moon, hyper-sleep, dodging an asteroid field and crash landing on the surface of Mars. The sustained g-force of 2.5 felt during the attraction is created by the centrifuge. The centrifuge is controlled by thirty-three show computers. Additionally, each pod can pitch 45° back and 25° forward and roll 25° to either side. After the thrilling landing on Mars, guests disembark toward the center of the centrifuge and out a large bay door. This door leads to a long hallway around the perimeter of the ride building where a theme song "Destiny" can be heard as guests walk to the ride's post-show area and store. The **Post-Show** area includes a children's play area and interactive games themed to space.

2006-Present: Feeling Green and Orange

It reportedly took more than 650 Imagineers more than 350,000 hours to develop **Mission: SPACE** over five years. In reality Disney hired the **Environmental Tectonic Corporation** (ETC) to develop the centrifuges for the attraction in 1998. By 2003 the attraction had opened and ETC was suing Disney over the project. Claims by **ETC** in the lawsuit focused on three primary areas: $15 million in damages for non-payment for work on the attraction, questions over who owned the development rights to the new ride, and **ETC's** concerns that the ride had not been safety tested properly.

Disney responded in turn claiming that **ETC** acted unprofessionally, failed to submit materials in a timely manner, failed to check measurement tolerances, and to comply with deadlines. Disney also reported **ETC** delivered defective and nonconforming materials, failed to manage the work of subcontractors, failed to provide proper document control and did not provide sufficient numbers of qualified supervisory personnel for the project. Despite requests for the case to be expedited because of the safety concerns the lawsuit lingered in the court system. Disney claimed **ETC** only wanted the process expedited in order to gain access to Imagineering's intellectual property.

On June 13, 2005, concern over the safety of **Mission: SPACE's** design became much more public when a four-year-old boy died after riding the attraction. A few days after the initial incident on June 15, 2005, a federal judge in Pennsylvania threw out the part of **ETC's** lawsuit that alleged the ride had not been properly safety tested. An autopsy released on November 15, 2005, found that Daudi Bamuwamye died as a result of a pre-existing, previously undiagnosed idiopathic heart condition called myocardial hypertrophy. The attraction continued normal operation after it was found that there was no mechanical failure of the ride system.

On April 11, 2006, Hiltrud Bluemel fell ill after riding **Mission: SPACE** and was transported to the nearby Celebration Hospital. She died the next day. An autopsy report released on April 14, 2006, noted that she had suffered a stroke linked to her high blood pressure. The attraction resumed operation as it had before, but this time the crowds were definitely spooked and staying away. Wait times for the attraction dropped significantly.

Disney introduced the **Green** and **Orange** versions of **Mission: SPACE** on May 19, 2006. The **Green** version of the attraction was to be the same visual and pitch/roll experience without the centrifuge. The **Orange** version would be the full-motion original attraction. The original standby queue for the attraction would become the **Orange** queue while the single rider queue would become **Green**. Guests entering the building would be required to choose which version of the attraction they wanted to experience and be given a card with warnings on it that they would be required to return to a cast member upon boarding. Signage was updated throughout the pavilion and the pre-show videos were modified to fit the two versions. **Bay 1** of the attraction was permanently disengaged from the centrifuge system and a second bay was reworked to do so according to ridership demand.

A lawsuit was filed against Disney by the parents of Daudi Bamuwamye on June 12, 2006, claiming that Disney never should have allowed a four-year-old child on the ride and that Disney didn't offer an adequate medical response after he collapsed. On January 11, 2007, the lawsuit was dismissed as the family and Disney settled out of court. Similarly the lawsuit between **ETC** and Disney was settled out of court on January 6, 2009. Both were confidential settlements.

The ride continues to operate with the **Green/Orange** setup presently. HP's sponsorship should be up for renegotiation around 2013. As expensive as the attraction was, it has not fared as well with guests as the less expensive Soarin' and Test Track.

8. WORLD OF MOTION

GENERAL MOTORS boasted that during the first year of operation its Epcot pavilion had more than eight million visitors; sometimes as many as 25,000 visitors a day. At that rate it was outpacing the park's iconic Spaceship Earth in ridership. It seems having a bit of foresight had paid out generously for General Motors – as they had eagerly signed on to be the first sponsor of EPCOT Center in December of 1977. The success of Ford at the 1964 World's Fair led to General Motors jumping at the opportunity to be the first company guaranteed an attraction in Disney's newly planned park. Their initial contract would be for ten years, starting with the park's opening in 1982 and running until 1992.

When the first contract was over GM's attitude toward the pavilion was dramatically different than it had been ten years prior. The attraction in 1992 was playing to significantly smaller audiences. The average ridership for the past nine years had dipped to 6.5 million guests per year – with the law of averages suggesting a steady decline and subsequently far fewer than 6.5 million guests in the attraction's final years. It is entirely plausible that World of Motion was seeing fewer than half the guests it had seen during its inaugural year of operation.

Worse still for the pavilion, GM seemed determined to see the end of the World of Motion. The press at the time even suggested that if GM continued sponsoring anything at Epcot they would not be sponsoring the World of Motion. Hero to zero – just like that.

1982-1996: The Original

As early as 1978 a model from WED depicted much of the transportation pavilion's design as it would come to be built. It very much had a resemblance to the earlier World's Fair attraction that it drew from for inspiration. The elevated upper portion of the circular building would be the main "History of Transportation" ride. There was also an exterior track akin to Ford's Magic Skyways attraction from the 1964 World's Fair, but this idea would be discarded for the time being. Architectural references to the 1970s would also be cast off but the general layout of the history based attraction would remain the same.

The World of Motion show space as it was built was contained within a cylindrical or wheel-shaped building sixty-five feet tall and 320 feet in diameter. The exterior was given a distinctive futuristic appearance by being covered in a sleek stainless steel curtain wall. Within the cavernous building the show space of the ride was an elevated ring on the second floor built around a hollow central core. The core itself made a sixty foot tall floor to ceiling continuous space in the center of the pavilion. It would contain the dramatic finale of the attraction called the **CenterCore**. The lower level of the building would house the **Queue, Load, Unload**, and **Transcenter** while the upper deck would contain the major show scenes.

The 1,749 feet of track for the ride would worm its way through the massive show space. There were twenty-four major sets that included sixteen full size vehicles, 180 animatronics (including seventy-three animals), and 3,375 props.

A wedge removed from the front of the cylindrical building created a covered **Portico** in which the queue would overflow out into. Above the extended queue the ride vehicles would make a swooping spiral out from the loading area around a mirrored column, then travel back into the building and first show scene. Guests would enter the portico space under the suspended vehicle path and turn to the right to enter the main ride queue within the building. The **Queue** itself was a simple series of wide switchbacks that turned up a ramp and met the moving platform for vehicle boarding at an elevated platform.

A nearby space was carved out of the first floor of the building for a pre-show exhibit from General Motors but never used. All displays were put in the post-show **Transcenter** and this area near the entrance was walled off never to be used. Overhead audio in the small queue space would play period-stylized orchestrations of the ride's theme song "It's Fun to be Free" by X Atencio and Buddy Baker along with the ambient sounds of passing vehicles such as planes, cars, and trains.

The ride vehicles themselves were an omnimover hybrid. The blue pod-like vehicles had two rows with room for three guests, or six seats total. These vehicles would travel in evenly spaced trains of three vehicles throughout the ride. Each vehicle was balanced on a central support column which allowed them to level and turn independently from the rest of the chain. There were 141 operational vehicles at any given time plus four spare vehicles available to swap out for maintenance purposes.

After loading, the vehicles would exit the building into the open **Portico** and guests would immediately find themselves suspended twelve feet above the ground on a loop of ride track. The vehicles would then circle a large reflective column in the middle of the space as they spiraled higher toward the first show scene. This loop, which brought the vehicles an additional twenty-four feet higher than the loading area, gave stunning views out into the park toward Spaceship Earth in the distance.

For the ride-proper, each scene would have comical sight gags juxtaposed against a very serious and contradictory narration delivered by famed vocal talent Gary Owens. This irreverent humor gave World of Motion a different feel from the other Future World dark rides. While the other opening day attractions were sometimes seen as being downright humorless, the World of Motion embraced a tongue-in-cheek satirical voice. The humorous tableaus found throughout the attraction were created by legendary designer Marc Davis, also known for his work on the Pirates of the Caribbean, Jungle Cruise, and Haunted Mansion attractions. Further, numerous scenes within the World of Motion were accented with projection screens – the first discernable sign of a shift toward screen-based-technology as a preferred method WED/WDI would use frequently in the approach of future attraction designs.

It is important to point out that World of Motion was a

huge building allowing for a large amount of show space. Calling it cavernous really understates the idea. This very well could have been its downfall despite there being many other omnimover-style attractions within Epcot. Many were on a similarly grand scale but it was World of Motion that had all the extra space. Space between scenes, space above scenes, space between the vehicles and sets. Lots and lots of open and empty space was a trademark of the ride compared to other attractions of the time. Spaceship Earth was wedged carefully into the sphere and the Universe of Energy went to great lengths to fill every inch of perceived space. Even later additions like Horizons and Journey into Imagination focused heavily on continuous scenic pieces and the envelopment of the visual field. In World of Motion the vignettes seemed to float on little islands in the void. The dead-pan delivery of the narration mixed with all the dead-space between scenic elements may have been the death knell that kept later guests away.

Ancient Times

The ride vehicles would re-enter the building from the portico into the second floor through a series of proscenium-styled arches and then be plunged into darkness. Footsteps could be heard as well as seen lighting up and spiraling up and around the vehicle.

GARY OWENS: Throughout the ages, we have searched for freedom to move from one place to another. In the beginning, of course, there was foot power. But with our first wandering steps, we quickly discovered the need to improve our basic transportation.

The first scene featured a pair of cavemen blowing-on and fanning their tired, sore, and comically glowing red feet. Animal noises could be heard coming from the surrounding caves suggesting perhaps this was not the best place to take a breather. Another note – humans depicted in the World of Motion were not realistic. They had an intentionally disfigured sort of cartoonish over-dramatized look.   They were certainly people, just weird looking people. For example the eyes of the cavemen bulged and the cheeks of the one blowing on his foot puffed out excessively.

The narrator would then chime in again to inform guests of "our first safe highway – water." Nearby an Egyptian boy floated on a reed raft in a papyrus swamp where a Nile crocodile lurked ominously. Projected images of various boats, such as canoes, rafts, and Viking ships could be seen in the background.

The next scene focused on mans attempts to domesticate animals. There were various caricatures of animals and their riders: an ostrich, an ox, an elephant, and a camel were seen being ridden with varying degrees of success. There was even a man atop a flying carpet. The goofy train of animals and riders ran up to a toll booth to enter an ancient dessert city. A man with an overloaded zebra was stuck impatiently behind a man holding up the line at the toll booth. The first few notes of "It's Fun to Be Free" could be heard over this scene – one of thirty-two versions played within the attraction.

The wheel gets invented in the next vignette and "Its Fun to be Free" would grow into a full choral rendition. In an ancient royal court the circular wheel is selected while a group of failed attempts including the square, hexagon, and triangle are dismissed by a guard. Projections of

112

various wheeled vehicles are seen: an Egyptian chariot, a Greek chariot, and a Chinese rickshaw. This of course transitioned to a Roman used-chariot lot with marked-down prices in Roman numerals. A shy and giggly woman also walked away with her newly purchased ride: a male Centaur who regarded her sternly.

Renaissance

Just ahead guests would see a large projected map with sailing ships being blown by winds across the Atlantic and clear off the edge of the world. From the water below the tell-tale humps of a sea serpent rose up and eventually revealed the head of the beast – peering right into the telescope of an eager seafarer. This began the age of the Renaissance.

The vehicles then entered the workshop of Leonardo Da Vinci where an impatient Mona Lisa sat posed and tapping her foot waiting for her painting to be finished. Leonardo, seemingly having forgotten the painting, works on one of his flying machines with an assistant.

Outside the workshop guests are treated to a scene several years later high above London. A man in a powdered wig accompanied by pigs and chickens floated merrily by in a hot air balloon that was snagged on a clothesline.

Steam Power

In the next scene a full-sized steam-powered stagecoach was blocked by an angry bull. The operators try blowing their horns to get it to move, but managed to only anger the bull further causing him to blow steam from his nostrils. Other steam-powered vehicles were projected in the background amid the sounds of horns and bells.

GARY OWENS: From hot air to the power of steam. Now nothing stands in the way of progress on the open road.

Steam boilers fade to paddle-wheelers and guests soon found themselves traveling along the Mississippi waterways. While the boat was being loaded with passenger and cargo another man-versus-animal battle played out as a donkey refused to board the ship.

Next guests would see how "passengers enjoy the scenic west with the freedom and adventure of the open road." Settlers with circled wagons hunkered down trying to avoid being killed in the ensuing battle. They were being attacked by Indians on horseback, as seen on a projection in the background. This scene transitions further west to the iron horse, a train, being held up by a gang of outlaws. The outlaws casually relieved the train passenger of their valuables while taunting the conductor.

Bicycles & Automobiles

"The peaceful countryside." In the not-so-peaceful reality presented guests could see one man was stuck up a tree after being attacked by a dog while riding his tricycle. Nearby another man had crashed into a mud wallow and was now surrounded by pigs. Various types of bicycles are projected in the background.

GARY OWENS: The call of the open road brings us a new wonder - a carriage without a horse. Yes, with the horseless carriage we thunder full speed into the twentieth century.

The automobile finally debuted in the attraction. Men cranked their model-T style cars to start them and in one instance in confusion succeeding to only lower and raise the canopy. Black and white projected footage of automobiles created the background for this section of the attraction. The motif of this scene progression was the idea that automobiles bring traffic and thereby subsequently caused the first traffic jam.

At a busy street corner a horse-drawn cart carrying chickens and produce had crashed. It blocked the path of an ice truck, a double-decker bus, and a red automobile. The scattered chickens clucked frantically and the produce rolled around on the ground. A man popped his baffled head out of a manhole in the center of the scene and the drivers all shouted back and forth in frustration.

Sunday Drives & Airplanes

The next part of the ride was meant to focus on the idea of people enjoying their freedom in their vehicles and the wide open spaces. People were out enjoying the countryside. There were joy riders and people watching biplanes in the sky. A patrol officer on a motorcycle could be seen hiding behind a billboard waiting for someone to speed past. People in a series of vintage vehicles, their wheels spinning and seemingly hovering in space, had come out to see an airshow and drive all around the world. There was even a family heading to Disney World with their son wearing Mickey ears.

Wide open spaces also took on a very literal meaning at

this point in the attraction as the tableaus became less grand and more distant from one another. Earlier in the attraction it could be said that the empty space was allowing a dramatic palette cleansing effect between the larger show scenes. From this point forward the World of Motion was a series of smaller islands in a void. Pools of light focused tightly on one large vehicle or smaller show scene in an otherwise empty blackness. Gone were the ground cover elements of streets, roads, and pathways. The full size vehicles did not help negate the effect that guests were starting to float through the static displays of a partially barren car museum either.

> **GARY OWENS:** Mobility is the byword of modern transportation. A way to move from here to there, for every need and every care. Now it's really fun to be free!

Speed Rooms

The vehicles would enter three Speed Rooms with curved wrap-around screens akin to the ones previously seen in attractions like the defunct **If You Had Wings**, **Delta Dreamflight**, and the still operating **Buzz Lightyear's Space Ranger Spin**. The effect of the screen wrapping over and around the vehicle combined with the right film truly created the sensation of high speed movement. It was one or the more notable Imagineering triumphs within the pavilion.

The first two curved tunnels would feature 70mm film clips of things such as a toboggan run, white water rafting, and a coral reef. The second room would have more abstract imagery with swirling lights, white circles zooming all around, and a seemingly endless field of white clouds rushing past. The third and final tunnel featured computer generated graphics of outer space travel and the stars.

CenterCore

Upon exiting the third speed room the vehicle would follow the edge of a massive scene called the **CenterCore**. This cylindrical shaped six-story tall model city of the future was the center of the entire pavilion space. Ride vehicles would circle the scene for 340 degrees. Trails of light zoomed across elevated highways amid sparkling building towers of dramatic height.

> **GARY OWENS:** Yes, our world has indeed become a World of Motion. We have engineered marvels that take us swiftly over land and sea, through the air, and into space itself. And still bolder and better ideas are yet to come. Ideas that will fulfill our age old dream to be free. Free in mind. Free in spirit. Free to follow the distant star of our ancestors to a brighter tomorrow.

After circling the **CenterCore** the vehicles would enter into a short scene before returning to the unload area. In this tunnel the pepper's ghost effect would reflect the ride vehicles as if they were futuristic pod vehicles with the riders within them. Guests would unload onto the moving platform and be directed into the adjacent **Transcenter** post-show area.

Transcenter

The Transcenter functioned as a post-show display area for the pavilion as designed by General Motors to feature their products and services. It took up the majority of the building's lower level and included various thematic areas.

Aerotest focused on aerodynamics and allowed guests to both see the working of a wind tunnel turbine as well as design their own car to test. The simulated wind tunnel section allowed guests to pick and choose different-shaped designs and see how well they performed.

Bird and the Robot was an Audio-Animatronics vaudeville-style show starring a robotic car-manufacturing arm named Tiger and his agent, Bird, in front of a projection screen. In the show, Bird is trying to get Tiger into show business. Bird smoked a cigar and spoke with a think New York accent. Tiger would perform various tricks at the command of Bird which showcased the agility of robotic arms of the time.

The **Water Engine Theater** held a film presentation viewed on a series of side-by-side screens in a small circular theater. The film featured the debate of various characters of the best type of engine – each character representing a certain engine type in the argument. For example a cowboy defends the internal combustion engine. Other characters speak for the battery-electric engine, the coal-fired turbine, the flywheel, the hybrid flywheel-turbine, magnetic levitation, the hybrid turbine-electric, the horse, and finally the mythical hydrogen-powered water engine.

An area known as **Concept 2000** or **Design 2000** later in the life of the pavilion featured a display on the design process for a modern vehicle – from basic modeling to computer models and final prototyping. This transitioned into the **Dreamers Workshop.** The workshop featured futuristic vehicles and designs said to be coming in the future. The prototype concept cars at the Transcenter were once the most photographed spot in Walt Disney World. Finally, **Concept to Reality** offered a showcase of current GM vehicle for guests to explore. In just a month a vehicle on display at the World of Motion endured between seven and ten years of wear and tear. This provided GM with real world data about how guests utilized their vehicles and which components would wear out the fastest.

Critical reviews of the new pavilion were at times harsh. In 1983 a review from the Chicago Sun Times said "Terminal cuteness afflicts this ride-through transportation show. Very young children may be slightly amused." It was rated 1-star on a 4-star scale meaning it could be missed without missing much. As other attractions in Future World came online the appeal of World of Motion began to show a significant decline. In 1992 the original ten year sponsorship ended. GM did not want to pull out of Epcot entirely but it had grave concerns over the World of Motion. It continued the sponsorship on a year-to-year basis until its final decision was made. In the end GM opted to continue their sponsorship at Epcot but with a new attraction replacing World of Motion.

Various props and vehicles from the World of Motion found their way to other attractions throughout the Disney parks. The sea serpent became a prop at Disney's California Adventure. The chickens went to Goofy's Barnstormer at the Magic Kingdom. Two men from the traffic jam scene made their way to Disneyland's Pirates of the Caribbean ride. Numerous other props and vehicles became part of the Backlot Tour at Disney's Hollywood

Studios including the hot air balloon, bull, and centaur.

The ride would close on January 2, 1996. During the final ceremonial ride with General Motors executives on board the ride system failed and was unable to be restarted. The executives had to be walked off the attraction – an ominous sign of things to come.

9. TEST TRACK

FEBRUARY 13, 1996, the GM Preview Center opened in front of the shuttered World of Motion pavilion. Test Track was to be a whole new attraction designed by Imagineering for General Motors reusing the sponsor's old attraction building. The Preview Center featured concept drawings of the new ride and a video showing a part of the computer generated simulation of the attraction. A large mural painted by French artist Catherine Feff was erected to conceal the World of Motion building during the long renovation period.

Early in the design process GM insisted that the new ride would focus only on cars – their core product – rather than the general concept of transportation as the World of Motion had done. As part of the original research for World of Motion back in 1976 Disney had toured a GM test facility in Milford, MI, while exploring concepts for the transportation pavilion. Because of this tour a portion of the original theoretical design of the General Motors transportation pavilion included a vehicle testing experience. It was a separate ride on an exterior track outside the history-based attraction that ended up being built. Guests would have tested the concept vehicles through an outdoor course but the experience was dropped when the entire pavilion was deemed too costly. The idea was to be resurrected in 1994 as GM mulled over their options for a new pavilion in Epcot. The new attraction was scheduled to open in May of 1997.

Much of the build and install process went according to the original schedule. The exterior portion of the new ride track was installed on time in March of 1996 without a hitch. By October of 1996 things were still running smoothly as the interior building renovation was finished and early ride testing began with a single test vehicle. Even February of 1997 was generally unremarkable as the show sets were completed and the attraction awaited the arrival of the twenty-nine ride vehicles for testing. Full vehicle testing was essentially where everything went wrong.

Two major problems became apparent during multiple-vehicle testing. First, the ride control computer simply could not handle the ride and vehicles as designed. The computer system would crash if only six vehicles were operating on the track at the same time. The ride control computer was tasked with accelerating and braking the vehicles to keep them evenly and safely spaced as they navigated the building. Due to the planned 65 mph top speed of the attraction precision was needed in the control of each vehicle. The programming as designed was failing to keep the vehicles properly space and would need to be dramatically reworked.

Further, the ride vehicle's tires were failing at an alarming rate. To explain: each vehicle has three onboard computers to help control the six brake systems and 250 horsepower electric motor drive. This drive system included twenty-two wheels that sandwiched the ride track making the ride vehicle not unlike a slot-car toy. The problem was with the four main steering wheels that guided the passenger compartment along the track. The strains placed on them throughout the vehicle course caused the tires to blowout frequently. Eventually Goodyear developed specialized 70psi slick tires for attraction to help alleviate the problem.

May 1997 came and went and the attraction did not open to the public as scheduled. In 1998 the Preview Center switched from the computer generated ride imagery to actual ride footage from a functional vehicle. The problem was not getting just one vehicle to work, but rather twenty-nine of them for capacity reasons. Stuck without a lot of options, Epcot management even began selling the original Test Track merchandise designed for the May 1997 opening from the Preview Center and Future World shops.

Finally late in 1998 the Preview Center was removed and the final ride entrance for the Test Track pavilion was built. In December GM executives were given a test ride on the attraction for final approval. The ride would begin Epcot cast member previews on December 11, 1998, followed by general cast member previews. Finally guest previews began on December 19, 1998. Test Track would be dedicated formally on March 17, 1999 – almost two years behind its original scheduled opening date. The question on everyone's mind, was it worth the wait?

1999-Present: The Original

After passing under the exterior track portion that curves around the cylindrical building guests would enter a newly created interior queue area. The portico from the World of Motion was walled in and is now home to Test Track's winding and elaborate queue. The general storyline of Test Track had guests arriving at a vehicle testing facility to see how prototype vehicles were run through their paces. The **Queue** reflected this testing idea by having a series of displays showing various vehicle materials being tested for wear and tear via repetitive test motions. Loud bangs and crashes were commonly heard in the queue area as various test simulations were activated.

Beyond the queue guests were introduced to the concept of the facility and their vehicle's controller in a **Pre-Show** room. The three pre-show rooms allowed groups of guests to essentially still wait in line while being fed the first part of the attraction's back-story. At the conclusion of the pre-show the riders exited into a small zigzag queue directly adjacent to vehicle loading.

Originally the rethought-attraction was designed with futuristic tireless sled vehicles. The design team changed the sleds to semi-futuristic cars designed by Albert Yu to be closer to real GM conceptual designs. It was deemed important for the vehicles to not be too futuristic looking. They needed to make sense as realistic test vehicles while also representing more than just one of GM's product lines. The final vehicle design seated six passengers in two rows. Each row would have a personal display reporting vehicle test results in real-time as it progressed through the Test Track attraction.

After boarding, groups of vehicles would advance to a

seatbelt check area. Passengers on the exterior of the rows wear over the shoulder seatbelts while the middle passengers have only a waist belt. Once everyone is confirmed to be securely in the vehicle the vehicle accelerated into the ride proper. While in the attraction the vehicle would travel along 5,246 feet of track and reach a top speed of 65 mph.

The ride began with the vehicles peeling-out and creating a smoke effect as it headed up a three story fifteen degree **Hill Climb**. This climb was located in what was the CenterCore of the World of Motion attraction. The vehicles reached a newly created third-level of the building and did a U-turn to coast down a similar slope through the first of two rough-road-surface **Suspension Tests**.

Once on a level surface again, the vehicle and passengers were sent into a demonstration of the **Antilock Braking Systems**. First the vehicle accelerated rapidly and tried to steer through a tight turn – failing and running over cones which defined the intended ride path in the process. These cones were designed to pop back up after each vehicle runs them over, but they rarely worked as designed throughout the life of the attraction. The test was then repeated on a parallel stretch of track but with the ABS reactivated. The second test was, as expected, more successful as guests could see on monitors nearby which replayed recorded footage of the two test attempts. These monitors also rarely worked as intended throughout the life of the attraction.

Next the vehicles were sent into a series of **Environmental Chambers**. The cold chamber was cooled to 40° F and the heat chambers lamps got up to 90° F. The final environmental chamber was a corrosive acid test. Robotic arms with spray nozzles attached loomed toward the vehicle while the control tower asks if the robots are shut off – presumably for rider safety – to which the controller responded "they are now" as the robots deactivated at the last possible second. An accompanying acidic chemical scent was piped into this area of the ride.

Next up was the vehicle **Ride Handling** test area. The ride indicated that the guest vehicle was cleared to enter Track Course A, as Track Course B sits alone and unused to the side. The vehicle maneuvers around a series of tight turns while accelerating for a fun bit of twisting and simulated guardrail grinding. This section was decorated with stylized road signs and intentionally fake looking cutouts of scenery. At the end, the vehicle passed a sign saying to turn the vehicle lights on – which ironically is the point where the vehicle turned the headlights off and entered into a dark tunnel.

Headlights of a tractor trailer blare directly ahead of the guests in the dark cave and the vehicle swerved to avoid it – seeming to hit the side railing causing sparks to fly. The ride controller remarked "That's what we call an **Evasive Maneuver!**" as the vehicle slows to enter the **Barrier Test** area. A loud crash is heard and a test vehicle in front of the ride path bounced as it appeared to have recently slammed into a barrier wall. The overhead PA system warns all personnel of a barrier test in progress and the ride vehicle turned a sharp right to reveal it was aligned squarely with a crash barrier in the distance. The vehicle stopped for a moment until the test alarm signaled and the flood lights positioned on the test area illuminated. It then accelerated toward the barrier rapidly.

At the final moment the barrier split open and the vehicle exited the main ride building onto the exterior ride track down a short drop. The exit from the building occurred where the World of Motion's invention of the wheel scene used to be located.

The exterior portion of the ride had 2,600 feet of track and roses from twelve to twenty-four feet with original planned top speed of 95 mph. The top speed was lowered during the design process to 65 mph to meet legal maximums and reduce the angle of the subsequent banked turn. Disney has remarked that banked corners greater than forty-seven degree would have made guests too uncomfortable if the vehicles were stopped on outside turn. Considering the complexities of the ride system this was a frequent occurrence. It was entirely common for guests to need to be evacuated from the outer-loop of the ride track after a lengthy wait. On some occasions guests had even been left outside in the rain – resulting in the need for what is called "merchandise support" to replace the guests clothing with dry alternatives.

The ride vehicle looped around the back exterior track and then began to accelerate for a straight shot parallel to the side of the show building. It achieved the 65 mph top speed and then entered into a tightly banked turn around the front of the building and over the queue entrance. The ride looped around nearly the full building perimeter before decelerating to reenter the building and gliding down a gentle slope back into the building. During reentry a thermal camera took readings of the vehicles passengers which were displayed on a screen above the ride path just before unloading area. Later in the life of the attraction a screen showing the on-ride photo taken just before the Barrier Test was also added.

Few other changes have been made to the ride since it opened. The corrosive chamber narration was truncated to a simple "um" in response to the question about the status of the robots. The pyrotechnic sparks from hitting the guard rail were removed from the evasive maneuver section. The barrier test crashed car became static display instead of the original crumpling and bouncing car.

Post-show and Inside Track

After unloading guests enter into an abbreviated and updated version of the old Transcenter. Numerous vehicles from the sponsor are on display and a small area houses what is to be a series of mini-attractions. The most notable of which were small virtual simulators called **Dream Chasers.**

While on a **Dream Chaser** guests would see what essentially was an elaborate commercial for GM vehicles and services. The arched single person vehicles of **Dream Chasers** featured small video displays and twisted from side to side in synch with the video. They would later be replaced with interactive exhibits on GM's eco-friendly drive system. After the exhibit area is a dedicated shop with GM brand merchandise called Inside Track.

General Motor's original sponsorship agreement for the attraction ended in 2009. They have since continued their sponsorship on a yearly basis until 2012.

In January of 2012 GM and Disney announced a new agreement to overhaul and sponsor the Test Track attraction. The newly designed attraction will feature the same ride system as the original Test Track but with all new show scenes. It will also be sponsored by the Chevrolet portion of the General Motors brand, instead of the full company. It is expected to open in the fall of 2012.

10. CommuniCore

THE TWO LARGE semi-circular buildings that flank the main plaza of Epcot's central hub offer 100,000 square feet of transient exhibition space. Various sponsors have come and gone from these areas in what has always been a very elaborate semi-permanent tradeshow. The original incarnation of these areas was called CommuniCore East and West – East being on the eastern side of the park and West of course being on the western side. Each side has two main buildings, the northern and southern sections. The southern sections, closer to World Showcase, have seen fewer exhibits than the northern buildings and by modern definition aren't really part of the same complex anymore. Rather, they stand outside the new Innoventions branding: the southeast building becoming Epcot's primary retail location and the southwest becoming a character meet and greet space.

For ease of understanding this book will focus less on exactly where within a building each exhibit took place and what exhibit replaced which and more so on the general phases of the overall program. When known, dates will be included in the descriptions. Often the general public was unaware something was gone until something else had replaced it.

1982-1994: The Original

CommuniCore generally had an open and airy feel. The large windows running the length of the buildings would allow natural light to flow in and the displays were crafted in classic Epcot themed colors: pale blues, purple, etc... An elevated walkway ran through the areas and guests would step down into the various exhibits which were in fact set partially into the ground from the building's floor level. Circular skylights ran above the main path and still exist today – though now out of sight in most areas of the buildings. They can still be seen clearly in the southwest quadrant. The low wall running the length of the path was covered in wall-carpet and topped with rounded and polished wood. Remnants of it can still be seen in the modern Electric Umbrella restaurant.

CommuniCore East – North Quadrant:

EPCOT COMPUTER CENTRAL by Sperry/UNISYS – A technology and computer-wizardry themed area. It was home to a larger show that looked down into Epcot's actual operational computer banks during the early years and presented information about the revolutionary systems via pepper's ghost effect. The show utilized the full two-stories of the space. *The Astuter Computer Revue* (1982-1984) was the first backstage show and featured the

"The Computer Song." ***Backstage Magic*** (1984-1993) was the second show and featured host Julie and her graphic sidekick, I/O. **SMRT-1** was an interactive robot that could play voice-activated guessing games with guests through a series of phones surrounding his kiosk. The **Great American Census Quiz** featured a continuous and accurate US population counter along with touch screen quizzes about census data. **Manufactory** explored touch screens in-depth and had guests assemble images using the feature. The **Get Set Jet Game** focused on computer controlled production and movement systems. The game had guests loading luggage onto planes by computer control. **Compute-a-Coaster** allowed guests to pick track parts for a 3-D coaster they could watch an animated ride-through of once assembled. The main show of this exhibit would close by October of 1993, with the exhibit area following in January of 1994.

TRAVELPORT by American Express – Touch screen booths allowed guests to explore various travel destinations and nearby representatives at desks allowed them to book travel arrangements. It was essentially a travel agency. It serviced more than 1,700 guests a day in its early years. It closed April 27, 1992.

ENERGY EXCHANGE by Exxon – The Universe of Energy's building design and ride format was not conducive to there being a post-show area directly at the ride so it was located across the walkway in the adjacent section of CommuniCore East. There was a giant model of a deep sea drilling platform and well as an oil well blowout-preventer on display. One of the more popular and interesting items was a 30,000 pound piece of oil shale

– the rock that burns. Numerous models of various energy facilities could be explored along with a coal locator which lit up rings to indicate which countries had the most available coal. Guests could hop aboard a video-bicycle and peddle away to see how much pedaling was required to create the same amount of energy as a gallon of gas. The answer was seven days worth of pedaling. Nearby a driving machine simulation explained how various factors such as air conditioning use altered a vehicle's fuel consumption. There was also a demonstration as to how photovoltaic cells worked and touch screen kiosks with information about a variety of energy related topics. Finally, a hundred-watt bulb was attached to a crank that guests could turn to get the bulb to glow. It would take a weeks worth of turning to equal one dollar of electricity. The area closed January 1994.

STARGATE RESTAURANT – Precursor to the modern Electric Umbrella restaurant in the park. It served typical American fare. The exterior seating area was under a series of unique umbrella-like awning structures flanked by a pond. The restaurant would close April 10, 1994.

BEVERAGE BASE – Located near the Stargate but functioning more as a snack and beverage cart than a full dining experience.

CommuniCore East – South Quadrant:

CENTORIUM – A large Epcot retail location with two levels. The first floor offered the typical theme park selection of plush, puzzles, and clothing. The second level offered items like electronics, watches, and models.

ELECTRONIC FORUM – A rare sight in modern Disney parks the Electronic Forum's plaza area featured live television feeds of news, sports, business, and weather information. Large satellite dishes on the hill outside the building provided these feeds. The thematic idea of the forum was polling and information sharing. The waiting area had kiosks allowing guest to vote for the person of the century and to get a private showing of any of the channels from the overhead televisions with sound. Within the *Future Choice Theater* guests were polled about various topics of interest and would vote their opinion by means of a selection pad built into the armrest of each seat in the circular theater. Results would be displayed in real time. It was later called **The EPCOT Poll.** The polling show would close March 16, 1991. The pre-show area would be renamed the **World News Center** and operate until it finally closed in 1996.

CommuniCore West – North Quadrant:

FUTURECOM by Bell System / AT&T – Functioned as a communications themed area and as Spaceship Earth's post-show. The actual building attached to Spaceship Earth was used as a guest relations area during this time. The kinetic sculpture of the **Information Fountain** demonstrated the plethora of communication media found today: televisions, radios, records, video, laser and audio discs, newspapers, telephones, traffic signs, film, books, magazines, and more. A large animated mural known as the **Age of Information** espoused, along with its theme song, the marvels of the modern telephone. As hokey as it was with the big wooden dolls the Age of Information predicted the coming of the internet.

Kiosks nearby were used to play games like **Phraser** where a computer would speak what was typed, as well as **Network Control** where guests would trying to route communications. **A-mazing Microchip** was a microchip themed maze and play area for the youngsters. The **Intelligent Network** was a massive 20' x 30' fiber optic map of the US showing long-distance telephone routes. The area closed January 1994.

EPCOT OUTREACH – The outreach was an informational area that answered any question imaginable about EPCOT Center or Walt Disney World. Pamphlets and fact sheets about many of the park's attractions were readily available. It was essentially the precursor to this book. The adjacent **EPCOT Teachers Center** allowed educational professions to get lessons plan for elementary through high school students based on concepts related to the park. It offered complimentary study guides. It was run by WDEMCO – the Disney educational media division and included a screening room for a/v information.

CommuniCore West – South Quadrant:

SUNRISE TERRACE RESTAURANT – Opened October 23, 1982. Counter-service dining offering chicken, seafood, and salads. Closed in May of 1994.

EXPO ROBOTICS – Opened February of 1988. A show featuring many robotic arms doing various tricks and stunts such as spinning tops on the edges of swords. Robots could also paint your portrait or airbrush a Disney design onto a t-shirt for purchase. Closed October 3, 1993.

11. INNOVENTIONS

FROM LATE 1993 to the spring of 1994 the various areas of CommuniCore were closed in phases as contracts ended. A whole new design aesthetic was going to be introduced and all of the corporate exhibits replaced.

1994-1999: The Original

The multi-leveled aspect of the buildings was demolished and filled in with concrete to create a single level floor. The raised walkways were removed and new access points were created for the buildings. In the main plaza between the buildings the reflecting pools were filled in to allow more guest flow through the area. The large windows of the buildings were covered to allow for more dynamic lighting of displays within the space.

The original curved entryways would be demolished. The West building would be expanded out toward the Living Seas and gain substantial show space. The shift in the ideology of the displays was away from the scientific and toward the home with personal computing technology. Innoventions was about what technology could do for the guest personally.

Innoventions East – North Quadrant:

GUEST RELATIONS – A major component of the overall change was the relocation of guest relations into the old CommuniCore building. It would no longer be at the base of Spaceship Earth allowing the building to have its own themed post-show area after the ride. The new location currently remains the same today.

APPLE COMPUTERS – Opened on September 21, 1994. The area was a general multimedia showcase for the company's products. It closed on January 31, 1998.

GENERAL ELECTRIC – Opened on July 1, 1994. The exhibit was a showcase of GE's home appliance brands. It closed on June 1, 1999.

GENERAL MOTORS – Opened on July 1, 1994. A showcase of future car designs including all-electric and fuel cell vehicles. It closed on June 1, 1999.

HAMMACHER SCHLEMMER – Opened on July 1, 1994. The area was a general gadgetry showcase from the catalogue company. It closed in September 1997.

HONEYWELL – Opened on July 1, 1994. Home appliances from the company were featured in this small exhibit space. It closed the fall of 1996.

MASCO – Presented a show called **Putting it Together.** The show had two parts: a tour of house of the future and magic house show. The magic house show would close in the winter of 1994, while the tour would last until the spring of 1995.

MOTOROLA – Presented the **Communications Dream Forum**. It opened in October of 1995 and allowed guests to experience freedom through communication and a virtual reality lab. It closed on May 1, 2003.

DISNEY INTERACTIVE – Operating from the spring of 1996 until September 3, 1997, the area displayed the company's video games on consoles for guests to try.

FAMILY PC – The interactive area opened in the fall of 1995 and allowed guests to send live messages and on-line photographs to neighboring booths or plan a future trip with printed details and appropriate maps. It closed on June 1, 1999.

ORACLE CORPORATION – Presented the **Information Highway** which ran from October 1995 to September 3, 1997. The area provided information about the new frontier of the internet, from home shopping to movies on demand.

ELECTRIC UMBRELLA RESTAURANT – Still functioning as a relatively simple American counter-service dining location, the Electric Umbrella did gain a second floor dining area along the breezeway during the makeover. It replaced the Stargate Restaurant in the same space. The exterior seating portion was extended onto the now removed pond and received the tarp-structure overhead.

Innoventions East – South Quadrant:

CENTORIUM – The Centorium continued to operate during the first overhaul of CommuniCore to Innoventions, only receiving new carpet and other interior updates. The second floor of the store in 1995 would become the **Art of Disney** location with figurines, animation cells, and artwork.

EPCOT DISCOVERY CENTER – The EDC would be temporarily located in the south eastern part of Innoventions near Centorium from the fall of 1996 until October 3, 1998 when it would ultimately cease to exist. See below.

Innoventions West – North Quadrant:

EPCOT DISCOVERY CENTER – After a brief stint in the Horizons VIP lounge since February of 1994, the EPCOT Discovery Center was installed upstairs in a new custom-made northern extension of the old CommuniCore West building on July 1, 1994. The new educational store, **Field Trips**, was installed below it. It remained in this location until 1996 when it would be moved to Innoventions East so the location could be converted into an **Art of Disney** store location.

AT&T – Displayed new technology like a wrist-phone and Sony's Magic Link personal computer.

BILL NYE, THE SCIENCE GUY – A small theater space introduced people to the concept of Innoventions. Disney had made up the word by combining Innovate and Inventions.

DISCOVER MAGAZINE – A display featuring *Technological Innovation Award* winners from the host magazine.

ECLECTRONICS – Hosted by Alec Tronic, an animatronic. He could mimic anyone and sang a ridiculous rap about the American presidents. The area featured numerous gadgets.

NETWORKED LIVING sponsored by IBM – This exhibit featured IBM's view of future living and computing through the internet.

LEGO DACTA - It was a prototype LEGO computer building program sponsored by Autodesk, Inc. It involved interactive LEGOs and computer controls.

SEGA – Largest of the areas, it included multiple video games and **Virtual Formula.** The racing game allowed players to compete against others at multiple stations in simulated vehicles in front of massive screens.

VIDEONICS – The exhibit focused on the home video editing services offered by the sponsor.

Innoventions West – South Quadrant:

FOUNTAIN VIEW ESPRESSO AND BAKERY – Opened on November 9, 1993. Split off from the **Sunrise Terrace** to create a small coffee shop.

PASTA PIAZZA – The remainder of the **Sunrise Terrace** was turned into an Italian-American restaurant with pizza and pasta. It would close by February of 2002.

WALT DISNEY IMAGINEERING LABS – Opened July 1, 1994, and offered a glimpse at Disney Vision technology, the virtual reality system used extensively at DisneyQuest. It used the Expo Robotics space and would close on September 9, 1995.

ICE STATION COOL – Opened in 1998 adding an igloo for its entrance to the main Innoventions plaza. A simple walk through icy caves with falling snow led to a polar themed shop where guests could purchase Coca Cola products or try sample flavors from around the world. Beverly made its first appearance in Epcot at this location.

1999-2007: Innoventions: The Road to Tomorrow

The grid layout and numerous areas within the Innoventions buildings were at best confusing. In 1999 subtle changes were phased-in to rework the areas and make navigating them easier. The Road to Tomorrow theme was established for the space and featured main walkway paths akin to the originally discarded CommuniCore walkways. Additionally a small robot called Tom Morrow 2.0 was introduced as the area's mascot.

Innoventions East – North Quadrant:

FORESTS FOR OUR FUTURE sponsored by TAPPI – The forest was an exhibit with numerous fake trees that showed how current technology was helping to preserve the world's forests.

HOUSE OF INNOVENTIONS sponsored by Panja – Another tour through a home of the future completed with Internet fridge and a robotic pet dog. It was closed by October 2009.

DISCOVER THE STORIES BEHIND THE MAGIC – Interactive kiosks themed to the *100 Years of Magic Celebration* at the Walt Disney World Resort. It operated from September 24, 2001, until late 2002.

DISNEY'S INTERNET ZONE sponsored by Disney.com – Promotional area for Disney's online presence and brand featuring interactive kiosks. It closed July 2007.

FANTASTIC PLASTICS WORKS sponsored by the Society of the Plastics Industry – Guests could learn that there was plastic in pretty much everything and then build their own plastic toy to take home. It operated from August 2004 until March 2008.

LOOK INTO THE FUTURE – Opening on October 1, 1999, this area had windows through which guests could see design prototypes that combined advanced technologies with everyday products. It closed February 19, 2001.

MISSION: SPACE LAUNCH CENTER sponsored by Compaq/HP – An advertisement for the forthcoming Mission: SPACE attraction. It operated May 2001 until shortly before the ride's opening in 2003.

OPPORTUNITY CITY sponsored by Disney Online and the Kauffman Foundation – More games and kiosks for kids. It featured a similar game to Spaceship Earth's *Power City* and operated from 2004 to November 1, 2006.

Innoventions East – South Quadrant:

MOUSEGEAR – Centorium became Mousegear and expanded into the now empty **EPCOT Poll** area through a series of phases. First on April 17, 1999, the shop moved into the old CommuniCore hallway which still ran behind the bulk of the store. The second floor and the lowered first floor pits would be removed. The redesigned and expanded location would open in September of 1999.

Innoventions West – North Quadrant:

ART OF DISNEY – This retail location opened in October of 1999 and essentially booted the **EPCOT Discovery Center** and **Field Trips** shop out of the building expansion which had originally been designed for them. The shop still resides in this location currently.

ULTIMATE HOME THEATRE EXPERIENCE presented by Lutron – A presentation of the latest and greatest in high definition sound and video home devices.

BEAUTIFUL SCIENCE sponsored by Monsanto – The area presented how Monsanto was helping to solve the world's food problems.

VIDEO GAMES OF TOMORROW sponsored by Sega – Video games, including the brand new *Dreamcast* system.

MEDICINE'S NEW VISION presented by the Radiological Society of America – A show presentation in a large dome that explained how the medical breakthroughs of today will change the way people live in the next millennium.

THE BROADBAND CONNECTION sponsored by AT&T – A game show where a telephone, television, and computer come to life to explore the world of broadband technology.

THE KNOWLEDGE VORTEX presented by Xerox – A presentation on the future of data storage, like how an entire book could be stored without paper on a tiny chip and the forthcoming e-books and devices that were much like modern Kindles.

ROCKIN' ROBOTS sponsored by KUKA Industrial Robots – This show opened in 2005 and displayed robotic arms which played music. Guests could approach a console and choose which instruments the robots would play. It closed in 2010.

THE GREAT AMERICAN FARM – An exhibit area with a bug tunnel for children to crawl through and a general interactive zone. There was also a multiplayer game called the **Great American Pizza Game**.

Innoventions West – South Quadrant:

FOUNTAIN VIEW ICE CREAM – Replaced the Espresso and Bakery with Edys brand ice cream in late 2007. The location had been operating seasonally until the change elevated its popularity.

CHARACTER CONNECTION – Initially installed as a test in 2005, the area soared in popularity as a centralized meeting location for Mickey and friends. It took over the old **Pasta Piazza / Sunrise Terrace** location. Its popularity is partially attributed to the large windows looking out into the west breezeway allowing guests to see Mickey inside meeting with other guests.

CLUB COOL – Replaced Ice Station Cool with a modernly themed club atmosphere in 2005. Gone were the igloo and snow.

2007-Present: Innoventions 3.0

Another aesthetic overhaul would come to Innoventions in 2007. The busy lighting towers that were found at the main entrances were torn down and the aesthetic in general changed to that of a blue and green motif. The Road to Tomorrow theme was discarded but the more centralized pathways were retained.

At this point it should be obvious that numerous displays have come and gone from these buildings. This was intentional. To prevent the displays from becoming dated – as CommuniCore had – the contracts for the sponsors of Innoventions were typically limited to three years. They also included a non-refundable $60,000 concept design fee to have Disney Imagineers develop an exhibit. The sponsors would then underwrite the construction which generally costs from $3 million to $5 million. Further there would be a sponsorship and staffing fee of $900,000 to $1 million during the three years the exhibit was active. In total these exhibits cost around $7 million to $8 million over four years.

Innoventions East – North Quadrant:

THE SUM OF ALL THRILLS presented by Raytheon – Opened on October 14, 2009, the Sum of all Thrills would bring Innoventions its first real ride. Guests would design a roller coaster and then be able to ride it virtually by boarding a simulator pod on the end of a robotic arm.

DON'T WASTE IT! sponsored by Waste Management – Opened on February 19, 2008, this area has interactive games exploring the trash recycling and disposal processes provided by the sponsor.

STORMSTRUCK – Opened in August 2008. This 3D film allows guests to experience the power of a weather event complete with wind, rain and lightening. After the first wave of the storm, guests use their knowledge to rebuild a home and prevent it from being destroyed during a second wave using a polling system built into the theater.

TEST THE LIMITS LAB sponsored by Underwriters Laboratories – An interactive kid-powered test lab showing the repetition testing for the safety of products that the sponsor conducts.

ENVIRONMENTALITY CORNER - Learn how you can protect and preserve the environment. Included an interactive paper-making station.

ELECTRIC UMBRELLA – The restaurant has received minimal changes since it was first renamed and rethemed.

Innoventions East – South Quadrant:

MOUSEGEAR – Continues to operate as Epcot's largest merchandise location. Minor renovations have occurred over the years but the general look and feel of the shop remains the same.

Innoventions West – North Quadrant:

THE GREAT PIGGY BANK ADVENTURE – A multi-station game where guests adopt a piggy bank and then go through a series of experiences to see how well they can save their funds for a rainy day. Opened in May 2009.

SLAP STICK STUDIOS presented by Velcro – A theatrical presentation with improve comedy that allowed guests to see the show *What's Your Problem?* and learn how Velcro can help solve their problems. Closed in 2010.

SEGWAY CENTRAL – Allows guests a chance to test ride a Segway Human Transporter.

WHERE'S THE FIRE? presented by Liberty Mutual – A multi-team interactive game where players roam through a house using a light gun to identify fire hazards on large screens representing various rooms of the home.

VIDEO GAMES OF TOMORROW presented by Disney Interactive – A constantly cycling display of video games from Disney.

Innoventions West – South Quadrant:

EPCOT'S 25TH ANNIVERSARY GALLERY – Occupied the space previously used by Imagineering Labs and Expo Robotics to present a display chronicling the history of Epcot in 2007. The briefly popular display closed with little fanfare in 2008.

FOUNTAIN VIEW ICE CREAM – Continues to operate daily after years of sporadic openings and seasonal status when it was a coffee shop. Apparently people like ice cream, even in the dead of winter.

CHARACTER SPOT – Replaced the Character Connection with more formal backdrops and a formal queue area with overhead monitors to entertain guests while they wait to meet Mickey and Friends. The success of the area has lead to the expansion of other character interaction locations throughout the parks.

Recent information from the group that works out the contracts for sponsorships within Epcot has suggested that new offerings will be coming to Innoventions soon.

12. The Living Seas

CONTRARY TO many people's assumptions, The Seas is not an opening-day Epcot pavilion. Long before the current Seas with Nemo and Friends version, the pavilion originally opened in January of 1986 as a spectacular futuristic ocean journey called The Living Seas. It was part of EPCOT Center's original Phase II plans. The pavilion was engineered and constructed by contractor Montgomery Watson taking twenty-two months to build for its sponsor United Technologies. It has 185,000 square feet of show space under its roof.

The pavilion contains, what was at the time of opening, the largest manmade ocean environment. The main building itself used 850 tons of structural steel and 900 tons of reinforced steel around the ocean environment, with walls that are at places three feet thick. The main tank is 203 feet in diameter, 27 feet deep, and holds 5.7 million gallons of water. It took twenty-seven truckloads of salt to create the environment and the water had to be drawn slowly from multiple wells to protect the water supply. The water is recirculated at 35,000 gallons a minute, the entirety being recycled every 160 minutes through 10,000 feet of underground piping. The gravel at the bottom of the tank is made of dolomite. There are sixty-one acrylic windows measuring 8' x 24' looking out into the main tank. They weigh 9,000 pounds each and were collectively the largest single acrylic casting ever attempted.

Several portions of the realized pavilion were far different from what had been seen in promotional literature, even from what the books Disney itself had published. A longer mythology based ride with a cradle of life sequence and Poseidon as your guide were dropped entirely. Drawing from the mass of conceptual artwork produced by Timothy Delaney a decidedly more scientific approach was where the story was to begin…

The Living Seas: 1986-2005

The pavilion opened with an educational film, the **Hydrolators**, and the brief **Caribbean Coral Reef Ride** (most people just called it the SeaCabs), all leading up to the main aquarium exhibit called **Sea Base Alpha**. The Living Seas' fictional Sea Base Alpha storyline was supposed take place in the year 2030. The pavilion as a whole strove for: "A better understanding of mankind's reliance on the seas, our past relationship with them, and the role they will play in our future."

The attractions within the pavilion were linked together in a cohesive guided experience. There wasn't really an option to opt out of any portion of the show as it was originally presented.

All guests visiting the pavilion would enter by passing the large mural of the sun setting into the ocean (still visible but modified for the Nemo version) and a rock sculpture with crashing waves of water. They would then enter into the zigzag shaped **Eel Queue**. This small darkened queue area was designed to hold approximately 350 people and remains today, modified and redecorated, as the start of the Nemo ride queue. Each turn of the queue would bring guests close to memorabilia displaying the history of ocean exploration. The oldest item in the queue was an illustration of the diving bell used by Alexander the Great in 332 B.C. From there guests worked their way forward toward modern times until they reach the Twenty Thousand Leagues Under the Sea's Nautilus submarine model and diving suit.

Every few minutes a group of guests were ushered into a large oval shaped **Holding Area**. The space was quite dark, and featured a continuous screen encircling the entire room just above the guests. This screen had a water-surface projection effect along its entire length that would be interrupted occasionally by a slowly changing slide projection of a countdown clock. This area would fill with guests from the zigzag queue and then present a brief message via slideshow from the pavilion's sponsor, United Technologies.

VOICE: Ladies and Gentlemen, United Technologies is proud to welcome you to The Living Seas. In a few moments, you will be entering the earth's greatest frontier: the oceans. Before your adventure begins, consider for a moment the accomplishments of those courageous pioneers who have come this way before. It was their insatiable curiosity and engineering skill that parted the waves for today's subsea explorers.

After the short sponsor message, a slide with The Living Seas circle logo would appear over a group of automated doors and welcome guests to the **Briefing Room**. This message would be displayed on opposite sides of the holding area depending on which of the two pre-show theaters was ready for loading.

The Seas Film

Upon entering the Briefing Room, guests found themselves in a fairly traditional theater space and were presented the film *The Seas*, directed by Paul Gerber. This seven minute film is remembered by most Epcot guests for its dramatic lines such as "and it rained, and it rained, and it rained, the deluge." The end of the film showcase a dramatic fly-through of a computer generated wire-frame model of the Living Seas pavilion which ended at the Hydrolator doors. The wire-frame image faded into an image of the real Hydrolator doors opening and the voiceover stating "Welcome to Sea Base Alpha" as the theater doors opened to reveal the Hydrolator loading area.

Hydrolators

The Hydrolator loading area was an intentionally sparse and industrial looking space with lots of fake overhead piping and walkways suspended over bubbling pools of dramatically lit water. The idea was that the three Hydrolators that lay ahead were in fact real elevators descending down into the ocean to a sea base (the first sea base, hence Sea Base Alpha). The effect was fairly convincing, as each Hydrolator would "descend" with an audio effect and cause the water around its supports to bubble up around the awaiting queue of guests.

Each of the three Hydrolators held a dozen or so people. Guests were intentionally packed fairly tightly inside and visibility outside of the space was simulated with a scrolling rockwork effect seen through small windows. Once the doors closed, the lighting inside would dim, the floor would drop slightly, and the rockwork seen outside the windows would rise up as bubbles floated up past the windows. The floor continued to shake occasionally and vibrate as an indicator panel inside the Hydrolator showed the depth of the passengers, and eventually their destination – the visitor level entrance of Sea Base Alpha.

Upon arrival, guests would exit out the other side of the Hydrolator and into the Caribbean Coral Reef ride's loading area. Many guests were quite convinced they had just descended several hundred feet and a few even complained of their ears popping from the change in pressure. In response to this, the Cast Members would simply open both the entrance and exit doors of a Hydrolator proving that it indeed went nowhere.

SeaCabs

A simple set of switchbacks lead to the slow-moving omnimover vehicles of the Caribbean Coral Reef ride. Essentially no one called it that because you had to enter the Living Seas formally to access the ride and you really had no other choice than to ride it once you were there, but many people did remember the one-off quirky name of the vehicles themselves – the SeaCabs.

Traveling at 1.7 feet per second the SeaCabs departed the futuristic surroundings of Sea Base Alpha's entry hall and made a quick right turn into a tunnel on the floor of the Living Seas' massive main tank. The tunnel had large acrylic windows on either side of the vehicles looking out into the tank and smaller panels above the ride path to look at the open water above. The tunnel was a direct route to the center of the circular tank. There it would meet the second floor main observation deck of Sea Base Alpha itself, swing another right-hand turn and follow the observation deck's walkway back to the edge of the tank. There the SeaCabs deposited guests into Sea Base Alpha properly. The ride was incredibly short and aside from the windows into the tank it had no show scenes. The journey was accompanied by the overhead audio of Commander Fulton welcoming you to the visitor center as well as radio chatter from different groups within the base. If you timed it right, you might get to see scuba-Mickey diving in the tank. Cast members reportedly hated working the attraction because the load area's control panel required them to hop on and off a small ledge that overhung the moving load platform. Falling was reportedly quite common.

Sea Base Alpha

After disembarking the ride guests found themselves on the ground floor in the center of Sea Base Alpha's visitor center. Suspended overhead was a full scale model of a Deep Rover one-man submersible, capable of attaining depths of up to 3,500 feet. The remaining area itself had the look of an underwater observations and research laboratory with hints of space age futurism. Airlocks separated different parts of the complex and the thematic areas were defined as various modules. The circular modules themselves were designed to look as though they were added in pieces and could be separated from the whole – like a space station. The sea base had two floors to explore. In the center of the large open space of the first floor was a Diver Lockout Chamber.

Lower Level:

DIVER LOCKOUT CHAMBER – The lockout chamber presented shows throughout the day of divers returning from the ocean or entering by means of the chamber. A long acrylic tube extended from the mechanics of the base chamber itself and into the ceiling of the pavilion. On command the tube would fill entirely with water or drain. This allowed a diver to either swim down through the tube to the actual lockout compartment and exit, or to enter the compartment and then swim up and out.

MODULE 1A – OCEAN ECOSYSTEMS: Contained a central display tube with Pacific Kelp that stretched between the upper and lower level. There were smaller tubes nearby which displayed phytoplankton and zooplankton. Symbiotic relationships were highlighted in an open-top Pacific lagoon, housing urchins, starfish and small reef fish.

MODULE 1B – MARINE MAMMALS UNDERWATER VIEWING: A large viewing area looking into the research tank which has shows up above on the second level.

MODULE 1C – EARTH SYSTEMS: A film presentation called Atlas which explained the ocean's effect on the Earth's weather conditions.

MODULE 1D – UNDERSEA EXPLORATION: Jason, a remotely-operated underwater robot, explains the role of robots and submersibles in the exploration of the oceans. Guests could also try manipulating objects through a JIM suit, an atmosphere diving suit which is designed to maintain an interior pressure of one atmosphere despite exterior pressures.

Upper Level:

MODULE 2A – OCEAN RESOURCES: The top of the kelp forest display from below extended up through a large opening in the center of the floor. Experiments were carried out at the Mariculture Hatchery found here.

MODULE 2B – MARINE MAMMALS RESEARCH: A Dolphin and Sea-Lion research center covering two levels. Communication experiments are conducted with the dolphins and video monitors show visitors a slice of the action above and below water. Primarily used to house rescued manatees later in the life of the pavilion.

MAIN OBSERVATION DECK: This large deck led to the middle of the main tank. More than 6,000 fish live in the manmade coral reef environment. Animals on display included dolphins, sharks, diamond rays, reef-fish, schools of butterfly and angel fish, blue chromis, barracuda, snappers and parrot fish. Diving and research shows made use of an overhead audio address system.

Exiting Sea Base Alpha was accomplished by boarding another Hydrolator bound for the surface. The same shaking and audio routine was employed in the exit Hydrolators as in the entry ones, but the scrolling rockwork effect was not used because it was ineffective in reverse. Instead a domed pool of water in the ceiling of the vehicle would light-up as if the Hydrolator was emerging from a deep darkened shaft.

The Living Seas as a whole won a prestigious award for engineering in 1987. The American Society of Civil Engineers annually recognizes an exemplary civil engineering project as the Outstanding Civil Engineering Achievement (OCEA). Established in 1960, this prestigious award honors the project that best illustrates superior civil engineering skills and represents a significant contribution to civil engineering progress and society. Honoring an overall project rather than an individual, the award recognizes the contributions of many engineers.

However, by the mid-1990s problems with the initial design of the pavilion became apparent. The salt water environment itself is extremely harsh on anything submerged within it, causing it to eventually dissolve, including the side walls of the tank. A company called, CH2M HILL, was brought in to design a solution. Special cathode ionizers had to be developed for the tank that removed charged particles from the water to lower the amount of corrosion. The tank became very technologically advanced, even envelope pushing. The company along with Disney developed guidelines to increase building longevity in Florida and other hot and humid environments based on their experience with the Living Seas. They showed how to create a climate which is sustainable through design despite the surroundings.

United Technologies is said to have tried to get out of their contract for the pavilion as early as 1991 when they abandoned their lounge and conference center within the pavilion. In January of 1998 United Technologies finally discontinued sponsorship of the pavilion. References to the sponsorship were removed, including the slideshow in the pre-film holding area. The countdown timer slides were extended, and one of the two pre-show theaters closed. When it was time to continue to the film, the remaining theater would welcome guests to the Briefing Room while the other side of the area's screen offered a direct passage to the Hydrolators for returning guests.

In 2002 the SeaCabs closed entirely. Guest exiting the Hydrolators were directed past the boarded-up SeaCab loading area via an existing bypass hallway and then entered directly into the side of Sea Base Alpha on the lower level.

As the pavilion lingered on without a sponsor and was beginning to show signs of neglect, the Atlas show in Module 1C and Jason in Module 1D quietly closed and the modules were boarded up in 2004. The areas reopened as **Turtle Talk with Crush** and **Bruce's Shark World**, hoping to pull on the popularity of Disney/Pixar's *Finding Nemo* film. While the Shark World play area was interesting, Turtle Talk became the star of the pavilion. The show features a screen replicating an acrylic window of the pavilion looking into a computer generated ocean environment. The character Crush the sea turtle from the film swims by and through the magic of advanced puppetry interacts with the gathered audience.

The show was designed as an early test of Imagineering's Living Character initiative and the guest response was way beyond expectations. As word got out about the show people began queuing up to enter the pavilion and many opted to simply hop into any open exit Hydrolator to backdoor themselves into Sea Base Alpha directly. Soon the barely-announced addition was on billboards advertising the park. The entire main floor of the pavilion became a zigzag of temporary stanchion poles with waits around two hours on a normal day.

Turtle Talk obviously needed a bigger theater space and Imagineering saw an opportunity to revitalize the whole pavilion. The entire pavilion closed in August of 2005 for a major renovation. By November 2005 the exit Hydrolators were gone, replaced with sliding glass doors. The newly christened Sea Base area was open to guests. Unlike its Alpha predecessor, Sea Base had been stripped of all vestiges of futurism and signs that it was meant to be a functional sea base laying on the ocean's floor. The walls were repainted in a metallic blue and many of the details of the earlier module and airlock design were simply painted over. Murals of the characters from *Finding Nemo* were installed and the remaining displays and signage were themed to the look of the film as well. The new exit doors functioned as a dual purpose entrance and exit for the pavilion allowing guests to visit the popular Turtle Talk while the front half of the pavilion was reworked for the next year.

2006-Present: The Seas with Nemo and Friends

On October 10, 2006, the refurbishment walls came down revealing the remodeled Seas pavilion. The entrance mural had been reworked to include silhouettes of characters from the *Finding Nemo* film while removing the setting sun imagery. The zigzag Eel Queue of diving history was redone as a beachside boardwalk leading up to a lifeguard stand of **Coral Caves Beach**.

From there guests would enter into the old pre-show holding area which was now converted into long queue area. The queue represents a journey underwater by use of special effects lighting and set pieces. Guests would then board newly installed Clamobiles vehicles for the main ride-through attraction which shares its name with the renovated pavilion.

The Clamobiles used most of the SeaCabs original track but also add an additional 280 feet of track. The ride took over the space that was originally the Hydrolators, their loading area, and the primary Briefing Room theater from the original attraction. The ride is still an omnimover, but the giant clamshell shaped Clamobiles face out sideways from the vehicle's forward motion. By taking over the old theater, the ride gained an extensive amount of space to tell the story of Nemo being lost in the ocean before reuniting with his father Marlin. The ride extensively uses projections amid coral reef formations to give the sensation of being underwater. Seeing as it was created at the same time, the **Finding Nemo Submarine Voyage** at Disneyland shares many of the same show scenes.

Notably, the entire tunnel through the tank portion of the SeaCabs ride is used but the view of the tank is blocked and instead a large continuous projection recreates the East Australian Current for a sea turtle encounter scene. However, the final windows into the tank are utilized with a pepper's ghost reflection to show the *Finding Nemo* character seemingly inside the tank with the real live fish. The characters sing the ride's theme song "Big Blue World" which was borrowed from the *Finding Nemo* musical stage show at Disney's Animal Kingdom theme park. The ride continues past these window vignettes before unloading in the same place as the original SeaCabs.

Once the pavilion was fully reopened, it was possible to relocate Turtle Talk into a larger theater space. A hole was cut into the rear wall of the old Module 1A and a connection hallway was made into what was the first closed and abandoned theater of the original attraction. Turtle Talk's old module space reverted to the typical tank displays previously found in the location but prominently features the old show screen at the rear of the area. It now shows a continuous screensaver of a digitally rendered ocean vista.

Overall the current pavilion is proving very popular with guests. Major changes are not expected in the immediate future.

13. THE LAND

ANCHORING the western berm of Future World, the Land pavilion rises up majestically out of the landscape and dominates the horizon. Having begun vertical construction in February of 1981, the pavilion literally cemented the foundation of Future World West. Reminiscent of a manmade mountain, the architecture of the massive 3,600 person capacity pavilion is often described as resembling both a volcano and gargantuan green house simultaneously. The Land became operational for guest previews on September 28, 1982, with a grand opening ceremony held on October 6, 1982.

The idea of a pavilion based on the Earth has existed almost as long as the idea of Epcot itself. In 1978 it was proposed as an ecology and mineral pavilion. No sponsor to be had, the niche was widened to allow for the inclusion of more varied concepts and ideas.

Early designs relied heavily on compartmentalized crystal structures with various tree-heavy ecological systems represented in the giant atrium forms. There were even plans for a rainforest ecosystem complete with treetop rotating restaurant. An attraction called Blueprint of Nature was to feature a balloon ride through the treetops. A drilling machine themed attraction would have provided a thrilling ride to the earth's core. The arctic environment was even to be showcased in the rear of the pavilion. These fanciful designs were abandoned when the original sponsor, a lumber company, pulled out of the project. This design aesthetic itself became the influence of the nearby Imagination pavilion with its towering glass pyramids.

1982-1993: The Original

Kraft Foods took over sponsorship of the would-be pavilion and the design was modified to reflect the company's involvement in the areas of agriculture and food production. Around this time the decision was made to integrate the temporary greenhouses into the forthcoming boat ride attraction as permanent fixtures. The **Kitchen Kabaret** show was added to bring greater emphasis to nutritional information within the pavilion per Kraft's request. Kraft's ten-year contract was said to be worth approximately $35 million.

The opening day pavilion featured much of the same layout as it does today. The entrance slope mosaic mural is meant to be indicative of walking through the earth's crust. Guests would enter the six acre pavilion, the largest in Epcot and comparable in size to Disneyland's Tomorrowland, through the second floor arriving in the glass-roofed central atrium. To the right was the entrance of the 428 seat **Harvest Theater** featuring the *Symbiosis* film. Directly across the atrium opening was **The Good Turn** rotating restaurant. Stairs and escalators invited guests down through the opening to the first floor.

The first floor was primarily the sprawling seating area of a food court called **Farmers Market**. The eastern wall, underneath the main entrance overhang, offered a selection of food stalls such as Soup and Salad, the Bakery Shop, Sandwiches, Barbecue, Potato Store, the Cheese Shoppe, Ice Cream, and a beverage bar. The western wall of the first floor was home to the entrance of the **Listen to the Land** boat ride to the north and the 250 seat **Kitchen Kabaret Theater** to the south. The small **Broccoli and Co.** store would open in December of 1982 to fill in the space between the food stalls and **Kitchen Kabaret**.

In the center of the food court's seating area was a large fountain sculpted by Jim Sarno with a mobile of hot air balloons slowly bobbing up and down high above it. The three original hot air balloons designed by Walt Peregoy were styled to represent the various food groups to help reinforce the nutritional theme of the pavilion under Kraft. The original pavilion had subtle blue and brown tones throughout. The most notable visual feature was a giant twenty-seven foot tall stylized sky mural in pale shades of blue and white along the atrium's upper roof designed by Peregoy.

Listen to the Land

As a precursor to the modern Living with the Land attraction, Listen to the Land was not all that different than the boat ride guests still experience today. Debuting with sixteen operational skipper-guided boats and two spares, the ride has always had the same 1,200 foot flume path. The differences lay in the selection of a few key scenes.

Listen to the Land began with a colorful and elaborate show scene called the "Symphony of the Seed" also designed by Walt Peregoy. Large set pieces on either side of the boat created an oversized plastic plant menagerie. The stems and leaves of the plastic plants would light up in pulsing waves in sync with the matching ride theme song "Listen to the Land" written by Robert Moline.

> SINGER: Just make believe, you're a tiny little seed, a tiny little seed that's reaching up to meet your need. With the right amount of faith, and the right amount of earth, you'll grow to see the sunshine on your day of birth.

This show scene, looking more like something from "it's a small world" than a semi-serious attraction about agricultural science, introduced the idea of the four seasons and the cycles of growth.

> SINGER: The seasons come, and the seasons go, nature knows everything it has to know. The earth and man, can be good friends, let's listen so our harvest time will never end.

This glowing cacophony of sound and lighting effects would be interrupted by the on-board skipper who then introduced the subsequent four biome scenes: rainforest, desert, prairie, and traditional American farmland. The animatronic animals of these scenes are said to have been remnants of the unbuilt Western River Expedition ride.

The boats would then, as they still do today, enter a large barn leading into two theaters with projection screens showing the past and future of farming technology. With an informational narrative from the onboard skipper the boats would float onward to the tropiculture dome to begin the futuristic greenhouse tour portion of the ride. The three part aquaculture cell and the thirteen bay sand culture building would follow. After the greenhouses, the ride would culminate in a scene which recapped the "Symphony of the Seed" before guests disembarked. A walking tour of the greenhouses, **Behind the Seeds**, has been offered since the pavilion's inception and is subsequently advertised as the vehicles unload.

Kitchen Kabaret

Kraft's Kitchen Kabaret was an audio-animatronic show in the spirit and style of the Enchanted Tiki Room and Country Bear Jamboree. In fact, the Country Bear Jamboree's Jeff Burke (along with Rolly Crump and Steve Kirk) is responsible for Kitchen Kabaret. Your host, Bonnie Appetite, began the show dressed as a simple housewife singing a sullen introduction song of "Meal Time Blues."

Bonnie would disappear as a group of condiments – ketchup, mustard, mayonnaise – known as the Kitchen Krackpots appeared as a ragtime band on stage. Bonnie would reappear dressed a showgirl to join the group in "Chase Those (Meal Time) Blues Away." This then segued into the emergence of Mr. Dairy Good, a singing carton of milk, from the refrigerator with an old fashioned radio-style floor microphone. He is backed by Miss Cheese, Miss Yogurt, and Miss Ice Cream for the song "The Stars of the

Milky Way." Next up was the upbeat "Boogie Woogie Bakery Boy" by The Cereal Sisters, an oats, rice, and corn-based parody of the Andrews Sisters.

The next act "Meat Ditties" was a brief comic interlude by vaudeville style comedians Hamm and Eggz. That led into the famous "Veggie Veggie Fruit Fruit" song by the Colander Combo and the Fiesta Fruit, with an introduction by Bonnie Appetite as she descended from the rafters dressed as Carmen Miranda. Once heard, this song is impossible to forget.

> **FRUITS AND VEGGIES:** There are no substitutes for we. Veggie fruit fruit. Veggie veggie fruit fruit. You see (can't you see) a balanced meal always wins with our vitamins, A and C. Si si fruit fruit. Veggie veggie fruit fruit. Veggie fruit fruit.

Bonnie would then thanks the guests for coming to her show as the entire cast reappeared on stage to run through a medley of their song in a dietary doctrine about the four food groups in the "Kabaret Finale." The automated doors of the theater then opened and guests would be deposited into the Broccoli and Co. store.

Symbiosis

The short-form *Symbiosis* film was presented continuously throughout the day in the Harvest Theater of the Land pavilion. It showed how mankind has both harmed and worked to restore the balance of the earth. It emphasized the symbiotic relationship between man and the environment. In theory, this "gripping environmental documentary" filmed in 70mm and directed by Paul

Gerber was the thematic centerpiece of the entire pavilion experience. A small plaque still sits outside the pavilion entitled *Symbiosis Between the Land and Humankind* that quotes bacteriologist Rene Dubos, Pulitzer Prize recipient, Rockefeller University:

> Symbiotic relationships mean creative partnerships. The Earth is to be seen neither as an ecosystem to be preserved unchanged nor as a quarry to be exploited for selfish and short range economic reasons, but as a garden to be cultivated for the development of its own potentialities of the human adventure. The goal of this relationship is not the maintenance of the status quo, but the emergence of the new phenomenon and new values.

Symbiosis was in turn the longest running attraction and last portion of the original pavilion to be modified and replaced.

1993-2004: Living with Nestle

Minor revisions had been made to the Land pavilion in the ten operational years leading up to 1993. The most significant of which was **The Good Turn** restaurant having become the **Land Grille Room** in 1986. Aside from new pavilion additions, much of the park was as a whole much the same as the day it had opened. In the fall of 1993 things began to change.

Kraft had decided to end its sponsorship when its ten year contract had expired. On September 26, 1993, the Nestle Corporation became the official sponsor of the Land pavilion. Renovation began almost immediately on

September 27, 1993. The Land became the first Future World pavilion to undergo a mid-1990s transformation.

Aesthetic changes were made to update the pavilion. The original subtle blue and brown color scheme was replaced with more vibrant tones. The atrium sky mural was painted over entirely and colorful banners were hung to help with the acoustics of the building. The umbrellas over the tables of the food court got new bolder fabric treatments and the floors got new carpets. The original three hot air balloons were replaced with five balloons representing seasonal weather. **Broccoli and Co** was renamed as the **Green Thumb Emporium**.

On a larger scale, each major area of the pavilion was to be reworked in phases. The food court became the rethemed **Sunshine Season Food Fair**, and the **Land Grille Room** became the **Garden Grill** restaurant – both projects were ready for the public by February of 1994.

Living with the Land

On September 23, 1993, Listen to the Land closed to begin its transformation. The ride reopened as Living with the Land on December 10, 1993. The elaborate Symphony of the Seed scene and its quirky theme song were removed entirely from the attraction. In its place was an opening scene of a thunderstorm in a deciduous forest illustrating how the forces that shape the land can at first glance appear destructive. A familiar voice, also the narrator of the original Seas film, greets guests.

NARRATOR: Welcome to a voyage of discovery and awareness of the richness and diversity of nature: Living with the Land. Our journey begins as dramatic and sudden changes are sweeping over the land. The approaching storm may seem wild and destructive to us, but to nature it's a new beginning in the cycle of life.

The automated narration would continue through the first half of the attraction until the vehicles entered the greenhouse portion. Updated 70mm film was added to the second barn theater. Once in the greenhouses, the onboard skipper would take over discussing the various seasonal crop rotations and projects of the facility.

The conclusion of the ride also had any trace of the "Symphony of the Seed" removed, leaving a fairly bland reentry tunnel to the main pavilion building. The final scene is a small lighted collage of people and produce from across the world along with a reminder that to succeed we must truly learn to live with the land.

Food Rocks

Kitchen Kabaret closed on January 3, 1994. Food Rocks opened as a replacement of the show with a similar format to the original on March 26, 1994. The content of the show moved away from the earlier focus on the food groups to nutrition. Pop icons of the era were represented in food-form singing parodies of their famous works. The show was themed as a benefit concert for good nutrition.

The parodies included Fud Wrapper, your host, who was supposed to be a representation of rapper Tone Loc. The U-tensils sung a variation of Queen's "Bohemian Rhapsody" to open and close the show. The Peach Boys (Beach Boys) sang "Good Nutrition" ("Good Vibrations"). Then there was "Every Bite You Take" ("Every Breath You

Take") by the Refrigerator Police (The Police), "High Fiber" ("Sledgehammer") by Pita Gabriel (Peter Gabriel), and "Vegetables Are Good for You" ("Breaking Up is Hard to Do") by Neil Moussaka (Neil Sadaka). A highlight of the show was a Cher-fish flying in from above and singing "Just Keep It Lean" a take on "The Shoop Shoop Song / It's in His Kiss."

Food Rocks was never particularly well received. Within the first eighteen months changes were made to Food Rocks to try and make it more appealing to guests, notably including a less busty Cher-fish animatronic.

Circle of Life: An Environmental Fable

As previously mentioned, *Symbiosis* was the last of The Land's three original attractions to be redone. It was closed on January 1, 1995, four months later than originally planned. It reopened shortly thereafter on January 21, 1995 as the new *Circle of Life* film. The film's new name and theme came from *The Lion King* franchise. It stars the movie's popular characters Simba, Pumba, and Timon. The decidedly more child-friendly film features Simba convincing Pumba and Timon not to greedily wreck the land for their own purposes – in this instance, building Hakuna Matata Lakeside Village while depleting the local resources.

2004-Today: New Heights

Work began to expand the offerings of the Land pavilion in August of 2003. Quietly a new building began to rise up between The Land and the Imagination pavilions. A formal announcement of the new coming attraction, **Soarin'**, was made on October 19, 2003. Since the attraction was being placed in a new building that was to be attached to the old building, the pavilion continued operations as normal until the closure of **Food Rocks** on January 3, 2004. The new entrance would literally be built right over the now much-maligned Food Rocks theater.

With programming of the new ride system already begun in late 2004, the entire Land pavilion closed for an overhaul on January 2, 2005. The new ride was so far ahead of the pavilion renovation timetable that it began previews on March 15, 2005, through an auxiliary entrance between pavilions while the main building remained close to the public.

The main pavilion itself reopened, two weeks late, on April 16, 2005. The entrance ramp had been dug up and entirely repaved with new guest traffic patterns in mind. A new color scheme for the pavilion was introduced with light tan, green, and sky blue highlighted by golden yellow. The hot air balloons were repainted to signify earth and the four seasons. The iconic central fountain was entirely removed. The up and down escalator directions were switched in anticipation of crowds flocking to Soarin'.

New seating areas for the rethemed **Sunshine Seasons** food court filled the space and became individually defined into sections by low walls. Each section had a corresponding seasonal color design including stylized carpet and tabletop patterns.

New food stalls would include an Asian Wok Shop, Sandwich Shop & Bakery, Soup & Salad Shop, and a Wood-Fired Grill Shop. The redesigned food court is noted for having upscale modern touches in both the food and presentation.

Soarin'

Soarin' had debuted at Disney's California Adventure in 2001 as part of that park's grand opening, formally named Soarin' Over California. Due to the popularity of the simulated-hang-gliding attraction in California it was planned to come to the east coast as a World Showcase addition for Epcot. However, a World Showcase location could not be agreed on and so Soarin' ended up being added to The Land.

Originally called Ultraflight, the attraction as a work-in-progress had multiple loading levels and vehicles on rails riding over an IMAX or Omnimax screen. This harkened back to the early designs for a flying or hot air balloon ride for the Land pavilion and possibly explains why it was placed in the pavilion when a World Showcase location could not be decided on.

Soarin' added an additional 58,895 square feet to the floor space of the pavilion. The long queue through the old Food Rocks theater is 800 feet from the entrance to ride vehicle, and 550 feet back to the main pavilion. The large main hall featured backlit photos of the earth's biomes with smaller cycling trivia screens beneath them. The seventy-four ton dual-ride system lifted eighty-seven guests per theater forty feet in air and into one of two eighty foot wide Omnimax domes. It simulates the sensation of hang gliding over scenic vistas of California. Soarin' was formally dedicated on May 11, 2005, and presented as a gift from the Disneyland resort to Walt Disney World as part of the 50th anniversary of the Disneyland park.

The pavilion has undergone some minor revisions since the 2005 renovation. The main queue hallway of Soarin was retrofitted with an interactive infrared motion-sensor based game system by PlayMotion SPG called Living Landscape. Five digital projection screens were installed along the length of the 150 foot long hallway, each measuring 11' x 25'. Groups of fifty people form in front of each of the screens and collaborate and compete in a series of custom interactive games run in a loop lasting twenty-five minutes in total. The success of the PlayMotion games has spurred the development of interactive queue elements for many older attractions by Disney's Imagineering.

Additionally in 2006 the onboard skippers were removed from the Living with the Land boat ride. The entire narration was redone with the voice of Mike Brassell narrating the full length of the ride. In the ever changing greenhouse portion RFID tags attached to the flume wall trigger the narration which is updated periodically to reflect new plantings and projects. On February 13, 2009, Nestle pulled out of the pavilion entirely and it is now operated by Disney without outside sponsorship.

Soarin' is currently the most popular attraction in Epcot and holds the longest wait times, sometimes reaching several hours. Along with Soarin', the entire pavilion remains quite busy throughout the operational day.

14. IMAGINATION

SPARKS OF IMAGINATION are not the only kind of sparks to be found at the aptly named pavilion. Sparks of joy and anger – sometimes rage – and even the tiniest sparks of hope can all be found in the story of one of Epcot's most endearing and infuriating attractions.

Few stories in life ride such a dramatic roller coaster. The problems leading up to the opening day were only the first of many hurdles the attraction would face. Since its inception the path for the pavilion has never been easy. A high was reached when it finally came together the first time – though months late it was a dream come true. That dream too would later struggle. It would fail dramatically when it sought to be reinvented. There would be triumph as it attempted to return to its roots. Still, it would fail again as partial victories only grant partial good graces. It lingers for now, waiting for a cue.

Should the pavilion be razed? Is the idea worth salvaging? Can anything be done? These questions are being asked as you read this and eventually a decision will have to be made. If there is anything the preceding history of Future World has made clear it is that corporate culture is not kind to unloved and sponsorless pavilions that desperately need repairs. So it is with great reverence that we invite you to explore the Imagination pavilion as it was and as it came to be – before the final spark is snuffed out forever.

1982-1999: The Original

Art can imitate life. Much in the way that the pavilion's host, Dreamfinder, would later explain that little bits of ideas can come together to create new things the Imagination pavilion as a whole was conceptually born from fragments of past projects. As the designers of the Imagination pavilion sought to find a metaphor for the process of imagination and the synthesis of ideas they began to borrow from the past. Architecturally the pavilion is a rethinking of the abandoned ecology and mineral pavilion. Though it would be polished down to a pair of stylized pyramids, the large glass-framed structures still harkens back to the sweeping atriums of the forgotten plan's crystalline structures.

The show inside the new pavilion would follow this theme as well. It would include a redrawing of characters originally created for the never-built Discovery Bay at Disneyland. Discovery Bay was to have been a sort of Jules Verne take on 1860s Americana with an attraction known as Professor Marvel's Gallery of Illusions. The gallery would have been an animatronic show akin the Carousel of Progress, but reversed with the audience looking out toward the sets. There they would have experienced a crazy carnival of creatures, and in particular, the dragons which Professor Marvel bred. During the conceptual design process for Discovery Bay a small model figurine was created depicting Professor Marvel holding one of his baby dragons. When Discovery Bay was ultimately rejected it sat around collecting dust.

Until 1977, when representatives from the Kodak company were touring the offices of Imagineering and seeking to possibly sponsor an EPCOT Center pavilion. In a moment of panic, brilliance, or defiance – it depends on who you ask – Tony Baxter grabbed the little figure of Professor Marvel and presented it to Kodak. Their response put simply: "Do we get the dragon too..?"

Soon the contract was signed and Kodak was photographing the little figurine and running it in full page advertisements. The whimsically detailed character and his dragon were juxtaposed to serious announcements of a forthcoming groundbreaking state of the art high-tech pavilion. Along with the more serious tone from Kodak came a request to WDI – make the dragon any color but green. Green was the color of the competing Fuji Film Corporation. The dragon became purple.

Steve Kirk who had worked with Baxter on the Discovery Bay concept refined the dragon character – soon to be known as Figment. The character design was handed off to X Atencio to be further massaged until finally it was given to Blaine Gibson to be perfected. Marvel himself became a bit younger, less gray, and a professor of imagination now called Dreamfinder.

Construction of the physical pavilion started relatively late at a mere fifteen months prior to the park opening.

While the Imagination pavilion was still a frame the nearby Land pavilion was nearing completion. The pavilion was designed to have three major sections: the ride, an attached theater, and a second floor post-show space. The ride itself was originally design to have two levels and unload directly into the second floor post-show. This version would have included a second turntable scene for the finale that matched the opening sequence but it had to be discarded due to budget restraints. The ride would stick to the first floor. Subsequently the first floor of the 128,200 square foot pavilion would be constructed first. The space frames of the pyramids would be added on later. Finishing and waterproofing the main building allowed the complete show sets of the ride to be installed earlier in the construction timetable. To this day, they could theoretically just take the pyramids off the top of the building while leaving the lower level intact.

The sets were in on time, but the ride wasn't working properly. The complex ride and show system was causing all kinds of problems – the ride would not make the park's opening day. Imagineering had a contractual deadline though to get the pavilion up and running. The attached Magic Eye Theater would need to be showing its film for opening day or Kodak would be allowed to walk away from supporting the project.

The film for the theater, *Magic Journeys*, was also running behind schedule. In a true moment of panic Mike Jittlov was given three days to shoot a temporary film to be shown in the Magic Eyes Theater that would introduce snippets of the partially finished *Magic Journeys* film. In the introduction before the film clips Ron Schnieder would play Dreamfinder for the first time. He would later be the first walk-around representation of the character in the park as well. This humorous film, though never used, depicted Dreamfinder frantically running around backstage at Disney attempting to get the film to the audience and explaining that imagination takes time.

Magic Journeys would open on time with the park along with the ride's post-show the Imageworks. The ride would not begin cast member previews until December and not formally open until March 5, 1983.

Journey into Imagination

Entering the pavilion underneath the large glass pyramids guests would find themselves in a stylized lobby. In the center was an elaborately decorated glass elevator surrounded by a spiraling staircase that led up into the pyramid atrium and the second floor Imageworks. Down below the walls of the lobby were covered in a magnificent mural depicting every scene of the attraction. This grand whimsical mural was detailed by Walt Peregoy and set the tone for the overall attraction. The ride's queue zigzagged in switchbacks of concentric circles radiating outward from the elevator shaft. Swirling colors extended from the mural to all the surfaces of the room and reflected from the mirrored columns.

The ride itself loaded from a curved loading platform and disappeared into a hole in the wall of the mural. The ride would have 1,460 feet of track. The ninety-two little blue vehicles were a sort of omnimover and peoplemover hybrid capable of traveling in a single chain but also breaking apart into trains while speeding up and slowing down for scenes as needed. This technical complexity is what had delayed the opening day and plagued the ride for the entire life of its operation.

The first scene within the attraction was actually a small screen which showed a silhouette of Dreamfinder in his flying **Dream Machine**. The entire concept of the attraction was based around a metaphor for how people come up with new ideas. The Dream Machine collected these ideas as it floated through space. It was styled akin to a Jules Verne blimp with a funnel at the front to capture ideas as they floated by.

The full extent of the **Dream Machine** would be seen in the second seen as the vehicles made a tight u-turn into the attraction and began circling a massive turntable. This seventy-five foot turntable was where the vehicle would remain for the next two and a half minutes of the attraction. The vehicles turned inward to face the turntable and continued to drift sideway along its perimeter while the introductory scene played out before them. In all, the turntable had five identical sets that the trains of vehicle would synch-up to. Dividers between the five scenes would come down and give riders the impression that they had stopped and were viewing a stationary scene.

Dreamfinder would introduce himself and then begin collecting and combining elements to create a new creation. The body of a lizard was shaded with purple pigment. He added in the nose of a crocodile, and eyes big and yellow. The horns of a steer were tossed in with two tiny wings and Figment was born. He sprung up from the rear of vehicle declaring he was "just right." To which Dreamfinder responded, "Not quite" and added a touch of childish delight from a birthday party.

The turntable had been Tony Baxter's idea as a way to implant a longer and continuous expository scene within an attraction. When it worked, it worked wonderfully, but it consistently had problems. The vehicles often could not adjust their speed to match the turntable and if the ride broke and stopped the turntable had problems restarting and getting up to speed at the same rate as the vehicles.

From the point after Figment was created the turntable show would continue with Dreamfinder and Figment discussing what they could do with all the things were collecting. Eventually the collection bag would be full and it was time to return to the Dream Port where ideas were stored. The vehicles would disengage the turntable and venture into the remainder of the ride as the Sherman Bros theme song for the pavilion would play.

> **DREAMFINDER:** We all have sparks – imaginations.

> **FIGMENT:** Yeah!

> **DREAMFINDER:** That's how our minds create creations. Right at the start of everything that's new, one little spark lights up for you

> **FIGMENT:** Oh boy!

> **TOGETHER:** Imagination. Imagination. A dream can be a dream come true, with just that spark in me and you.

This theme would be repeated and have appropriate variations played for the subsequent portions of the ride. In the next scene guests were introduced to the **Dream Port** where ideas were stores and synthesized into new things. The scene was very industrial looking with gears and valves and other gadgetry strewn about. Meters indicated if the Dream Port's containers were full, empty, etc... The collection of ideas included things like a swirling brainstorm, a holographic deep thought container, and a box full of clapping hands. There were even actual barrels of laughs and musical notes on perches representing song birds. Eventually guests would see over seventy-eight special effects in the attraction. It was a pun-filled sight-gag heaven. Toward the end of this sequence a perfume bottle would spray Morning Mist from a smellitizer cannon that filled the air with the scent of fresh flowers.

The next section of the ride was dedicated to concepts of art. Spouts would pour out sun rays, lava, and gem stones which Dreamfinder would use with a giant brush to paint a giant mural that came to life with color as the vehicles passed by. Large origami animals going around on a carousel dominated the next portion of the scene. They were stark white and highly stylized. This memorable portion of the attraction was said to also be the work of Walt Peregoy, based on his ideas of abstract imagery in ever-changing line and form. In a small pond nearby Figment is seen painting color onto the white scenery around him from a pot of gold that released a rainbow.

The white flowers and foliage gave way to cloud shapes as guests entered the literature portion of the ride. Lighting flashed across the clouds and thunder was heard in the air as Dreamfinder sat at a pipe organ playing a tune. The organ itself was styled like a volcano and spewed out words like "shake" and "surprise" that then became the structure of the scenery itself.

Nearby Figment was holding letter-blocks that spelled the word "bat" and a shadow behind him showed bats flapping in the wind. He spun a block and the word became "cat" and the shadow behind him changed to the silhouette of a cat with its back arched. The aforementioned pipe organ words piled up structurally ahead in a large rock formation. They created an arch the vehicles would travel under. The word "shake" rumbled above while "tumble" cascaded down the side. Loud crashing sounds were heard as the vehicle passed under the arch and the word "surprise" lit up on the wall ahead.

The craggy area gave way to stacks of books that took on the characteristics of their titles. The phrase "Once upon a time…" led up a path to a castle whose plume of smoke spelled out "fairytale." Further down books of vampires and nightmares threatened the passing guests but Figment held the book of monsters closed.

Leaving the frightening world of literature guests were brought to the backstage area of a theater. Figment with tux and top hat prepared for the show in front of a traditional makeup mirror. Together with Dreamfinder he sang a verse about putting on a show as Dreamfinder conducted an orchestra of laser lights. The lasers created various shapes and designs, and as an aside, were just running a test program that came with the laser projection system when Disney purchased it. Disney had worked on reprogramming the system to make a Figment shaped laser drawing but when push came to shove the default display was used.

Amid a field of stars Figment was dressed as an astronaut and tried to hitchhike his way along with the guests to the next scene.

DREAMFINDER: What about science?

The science and technology scene was possibly the most impressive in the whole attraction. In the center of a circular room Dreamfinder stood operating some sort of controls by spinning a winch. The controls were attached to massive microscope/telescope looking into a large clear orb. Six screens around the room displayed the magnified imagery of water, time-shifted plant growth, space, crystals, and tiny organisms. The vehicles then traveled behind the microscope/telescope where Figment was seen bouncing around inside the device.

A flash of light temporarily blinded guests as their picture is taken. Figment was seen at a crystal ball wearing a genie hat and waving his arms. It was at this point Figment realized that he could harness the power of imagination to create new things. The vehicles entered into another scene flanked with screens with Figment in the center conducting the various screens together in song. The screens were filled with images of Figment doing many things: dancing on a stage, flying through the sky like a super hero, weight lifting, acting like a scientist, mountain climbing, being a cowboy by riding a wooden horse, sailing, and as a pirate sitting on a treasure chest in the ocean.

The film motif is continued in the next scene where Dreamfinder was behind a film camera and the earlier guest photographs were shown on a screen. Dreamfinder bid riders farewell and invited them to enjoy the Imageworks.

DREAMFINDER: And what about you folks? Imagination is something that belongs to all of us. So, join us now in a magical playground, where technology and your creativity combine to make dazzling new images. Next stop, the Image Works!

The vehicles would then reach the unload platform which originally was a moving platform. However, due to the ride vehicles changing speed throughout the ride they tended not to arrive at the station in-synch with the unload platform. This caused problems with the platform to the point where it was turned off shortly after the ride opened and removed entirely by 1991. Guests were assisted in stepping carefully out of the moving vehicles onto the stationary surface. A short walk down a brightly painted hallway later the guests would find themselves back in the original lobby and able to ascend the stairs to the Imageworks.

Imageworks

By heading up the spiral staircase or taking the glass elevator guests were brought up to the atrium inside the larger of the two glass pyramids. Early plans for the area included an exterior balcony outside the pyramids but the idea was eventually dropped prior to construction. The atrium space itself was mostly just open space and modestly appointed with small plants. It offered stunning views out into the park toward Spaceship Earth.

Heading into the building and under the smaller pyramid structure guests could enter what was a first ever of its type creative and interactive area. The playground of the Imageworks would be a model for all such exhibits from Disney and museums and other theme park operators. The 18,500 square feet of the Imageworks included numerous activities:

THE SENSOR MAZE: The premise of the sensor maze was that it knew you were there and reacted. The Rainbow

Corridor that served as the entrance had two modes of operation. It could either run a constant changing cascade of colored neon arches or it could assign each guest that entered a color and have the color follow them for the length of the tunnel. Beyond the entrance tunnel there was a room where panels in the floor activated mirrors that would warp guests' reflections. The mirrors were made of a flexible reflective plastic that vibrated when the panels in the floor were stood on along with strobe lights and sound effects. Next a large orb called Lumia reacted to the sound of guests' voices with a light show. Finally the Stepping Tones had pools of light that made sounds when stepped on. Pressure pads in the floor made with GE brand Lexan sheets triggered a speaker and colored spotlight above each pool. To exit guests had to walk past a Digital Wall that created a diffused mosaic image of their shadow.

DREAMFINDER'S SCHOOL OF DRAMA: Utilized three chromakey screens to let guests act out a scene from a fictional film and then be superimposed onto the playback. Originally there were choices of being in a western, sci-fi, or fairytale scene.

MAGIC PALETTE: Fourteen booths along the rear wall allowed guests to use light pens – revolutionary technology in the early 80s – to draw and color images on a screen digitally.

LIGHT WRITER: Four stations where guests could make patterns with lasers on a wall.

KALEIDOSCOPE: Giant wall mounted kaleidoscopes with patterns controlled by guests.

PIN TABLES: Guests could push up on thousands of identical pins in each table to create swirling patterns. There were five tables total.

ELECTRONIC PHILHARMONIC: Guests could move their hands through light beams to make music and trigger special effects. The system used a sonar sensor to detect the arm movements of up to six guests, but the light beams were just for show.

BUBBLE MUSIC: A series of pads on a console when pressed opened valves that made bubbles in a tank of color liquid and played a sound. The tanks of liquid were in front of a projector that cast a pattern onto the wall of the smaller pyramid. Guests could mix up to six colors in the image.

By the 1990s the Imageworks was updated. Some areas were removed, some were replaced entirely, while others were merely renamed.

FIGMENTS COLORING BOOK: Replaced Bubble Music using the same general concept of creating colorful patterns on defined spaces on the wall. The updated version had white images to color-in using a paintbrush pointer gun.

DREAMFINDER'S SCHOOL OF DRAMA: Became a single stage and replaced the Digital Wall by taking over its location at the exit of the Sensor Maze.

MAKING FACES: This addition allowed guest to alter a digital image of themselves at touch screen kiosks in the area previously occupied by the school of drama. Guests could add cartoon eyes, ears, etc… to their faces.

THE SENSOR MAZE: Within the maze the vibrating mirror room was bypassed and Mirage replaced Lumia. Mirage had cylindrical columns with 3D figment animations. If guests tried to touch the image it would disappear.

DREAMFINDER'S RACE: Five anamorphic discs spinning at different speeds with various balloon vehicles "racing" under a glass table. A central mirrored column reflected the discs so they appeared to be floating. The display was topped with a glowing crystal structure.

After visiting the Imageworks guests would take an escalator down to the first level of the pavilion which deposited them directly into the queue for the nearby Magic Eye Theater. Together the various attractions could take more than two hours of a guest's day to explore if they followed the implied progression. Most did.

Magic Journeys

Magic Journeys was the first film shown in the 592 seat Magic Eye Theater. The seventeen minute film chronicled the journey of the mind and how the mind sparks into different worlds and places seemingly at random. Children exploring the world were used to frame the concept and guests were presented with their sights and thoughts in 3D. It was the first time high speed shots were used in 3D. It also had remarkable quality of color and image sharpness. The seventy-five frames per second of the film were well above the typical twenty-four frames of most films. The 65mm exposure allowed for sharper images than previously produced in 3D. The projectors themselves were mounted on rigs allowing them to move back and forth to change the perceived depth as the film was presented. The film was directed by Murray Lerner. The camera rig to shoot the film was developed by Steve Hines of WED along with Eastman Kodak. Paul Ryan served as the director of photography on the project. The film closed on February 9, 1986, and was sent to the Magic Kingdom for a run in Fantasyland.

1986-1994: *Captain EO*

On September 12, 1986, a new 3D film called *Captain EO* starring Michael Jackson opened in the Magic Eye Theater. The film cost over $17 million to produce, making it the most costly film per minute. It works out to be about one million dollars per minute of film. Lucasfilm provided more than 150 special effects for the seventeen minute movie. The film, which told the story of star-traveling Captain EO and his ragtag crew as they saved the universe proved extremely popular when it first opened. The popularity eventually waned and the film, which was really just an extended Michael Jackson music video, became viewed as stale by most guests. On July 11, 1994 it would close.

1994-2010: *Honey, I Shrunk the Audience*

On November 24, 1994, a new film based on the popular *Honey I Shrunk the Kids* franchise opened in the Magic Eye Theater. The film would introduce multiple in-theater special effects to the space such as sprays of water and heel-whip effects. It would be billed as a 4D experience. The plot centered on the concept of the franchise's star Wayne Szalinski receiving the Inventor of the Year award from the Imagination Institute. The film introduced the Imagination Institute theme to the pavilion. While demonstrating his inventions Wayne would unwittingly cause something to go wrong – in this case he shrunk the audience. The theater floor also received a motion base as part of the upgrades for the film and would wobble and tremble as people walked around it in its shrunken state for much of the film. Eventually the day would be saved and guests would be returned to their normal size.

Like all franchise based attractions the popularity of *Honey I Shrunk the Audience* would eventually taper off and the crowds would become sparse, but not before the film could do some serious damage to the adjacent attraction.

1999-2001: Journey into YOUR Imagination

If ever there was a dreadful idea for an attraction backed by shoddy logic and poor decision making this would be it. With the popularity of *Honey I Shrunk the Audience* the pavilion's management decided to reroute the queue of the Magic Eye Theater to essentially block off the entrance to Journey into Imagination. Guests were instead routed directly to the Magic Eye rather than the previously design path of the ride, then the post-show, and then the film. Because the film exits into a courtyard design to move large groups of people out and away from the pavilion, guests would just leave rather than return to navigate around the queue for the film to find the entrance to the ride.

Attendance dropped dramatically at the ride despite it still having stellar guest ratings. Instead of seeing the problem of the reformatted queue the park's management felt it was time to update the ride because people were losing interest. They used it as leverage during the renegotiations of the pavilion's sponsorship with Kodak to get them to finance a new ride. The original Journey into Imagination closed October 10, 1998.

Within the pavilion demolition and construction crews went to work. The open atrium at the entrance lobby would be walled in and separated. The spiral staircase and elevator would become part of a new post-show and retail area. The upstairs Imageworks itself would be simply shut off and ignored – none of the second floor would be utilized in the new pavilion design. Having the guests on a single floor of the building would allow for lower insurance and maintenance costs in the pavilion. A large portion of the original ride path would be covered over to carve out space for the 5,000 square foot post-show downstairs. In particular the Flight to Imagination turntable scene would be completely removed with a small track piece added to bypass its portion of the track entirely. The new link shortened the original ride path by 40%.

The mural at the entrance was painted over along with the exterior being given a new garish orange color scheme instead of the original soft purple and blue. The entrance to the new queue space would be through the same hole that the vehicles used to enter into the old ride. The new loading area would be right in the center of the old Flight to Imagination scene. The original escalator coming down from the Imageworks and loading into the Magic Eye

Theater would be boxed in and blocked off. Guests would now have to go outside the pavilion to be able to access the Magic Eye Theater.

The new ride itself could really best be described as awful. It was built as an extension of the *Honey I Shrunk the Audience* film where the ride itself now functioned as the Imagination Institute. Guests were invited inside to have their imagination measured and tested. The ride stated in the first scene that guests' minds were full of nothingness. Dr. Nigel Channing from the film next door was now the host of the "open house" tour of the institute. Guests lacking imagination were to be put through a series of experiments to increase their imagination. Guest feedback ranged from "Ok" to "Awful." Disney's CEO Michael Eisner rode the new Journey into Your Imagination on November 1, 1999, and immediately ordered a $5 million overhaul. The ride closed October 8, 2001, but the damage had already been done to the physical structure of the attraction.

2002-Present: Journey into Imagination with Figment

The initial $5 million proposed by Eisner quickly grew into a complete rebuild of a majority of the ride. Seven new show scenes were installed. The upside-down scene, sound room, and finale drop walls were the extent of what was kept with minor tweaking. The rest was torn out and thrown on the trash heap where it belonged. Figment was re-added as a co-host to the attraction along with Dr. Nigel Channing. Imagineering salvaged as many of the old ride's original Figment animatronics as they could find. The new ride had the same track length as the previous abomination but added two extra show stops to increase to the total length of the attraction. Soft openings for the new-new ride began in April of 2002 with the ride opening to the public June 1, 2002.

The ride has remained generally unchanged since then. The downstairs version of the Imageworks that was established during the last version of the attraction has continued to operate with a modified version of the Stepping Tones, Making Faces, and Electronic Philharmonic. Most fans of the original pavilion agree the simple effects of the original versions of these interactivities lost their charm in the modern translations.

In 2010 *Honey I Shrunk the Audience* finally was proven poor enough in popularity that something had to be done to keep the theater from becoming a ghost town. It was closed in May of 2010. Due to the recent resurgence of the popularity of Michael Jackson after his death the film *Captain EO* was returned to the theater. It re-opened on July 2, 2010, and proved that Imagineering can indeed go back and revive a dead attraction successfully.

In the fall of 2010 Kodak dropped their sponsorship of the pavilion. The future of the pavilion is currently unknown but there is hope for something better on the horizon.

15. FUTURE WORLD MISC

THERE ARE a few tidbits worth mentioning about the Future World area of the park that do not fit cleanly into the discussion of the various pavilions.

Millennium Celebration

At the entrance of the park thirty massive stone monuments were erected as part of the Millennium Celebration in 1999 for a monument called Leave a Legacy. Small etched-aluminum tiles to be mounted on the stones were sold as a souvenir to guests. The theory being that the smiling faces of guests etched onto the metal would be an endearing legacy of that moment in time. The stone monuments themselves took a major restructuring of the entrance plaza to install. Numerous planters and the organic feeling of the entryway were lost. Additionally the central fountain in front of Spaceship Earth was restyled to match the monuments and lost its three distinctive acrylic pillars that had existed since the park opened.

Original plans were for an audio-animatronic figure of the Millennium Celebration's host, the Sage of Time, to stand in their place in the center of the fountain and welcome guests. The idea was cut despite the fountain being modified to match the new look of the surrounding area. The pillars were sold off on eBay in the early 2000s and the center of the fountain has remained barren except when used for a topiary stand during the yearly Flower and Garden Festivals.

Also for the Millennium Celebration a massive Mickey Mouse hand holding a wand was erected over Spaceship Earth that spelled out the year 2000 in ribbon-like numerals above the geosphere covered in hundreds of glittering eye catchers. Matching stars were affixed between the joints of Spaceship Earths facet panels. Further into the park the Innoventions plaza was restyled with a pin cart located prominently behind Spaceship Earth and a series of triangular tarps anchoring into the pin cart looming over the plaza to create the millennium-circus look.

While most people enjoyed these additions for the duration of the Millennium Celebration from 1991 to 2001, they quickly wore out their welcome as the new century wore on. The wand's message was quickly changed to read Epcot instead of 2000 in 2001. Still, guests wanted it gone after the celebration was over. Despite the complaints the wand persisted until 2007 when it was finally torn down – years in advance of the intended demolition date. Guest complaints about the unsightly tower had finally won out.

The Leave a Legacy monoliths still remain in the park as do the plaza tarps. Neither is particularly well liked, but Leave a Legacy has the burden of being a business failure as well. Due to a lack of interest in sales Disney abandoned selling the tiles on the monoliths on June 16, 2007. Disney commented at the time that the program had sold 550,000 tiles over the life of the program.

The problem though, was that Disney fan have long memories and soon dug out the original literature for the monument. The stones were designed to hold 750,000 images. That meant that in the eight years the program had run Disney still had 200,000 empty tiles they were unable to fill despite numerous promotions and giveaways that essentially made the stones free to park guests. A good number of people simply did not want them and the truth of the matter is obvious by looking at the number of blank stones still in the courtyard.

The contract for the original tiles states that Disney has the right to relocate them at any time at their discretion to another area of the Walt Disney World property. Further, the images could be removed on or after the twentieth anniversary of the original installation. Many fans of the park anxiously wait for one or the other to occur.

Odyssey

Between the Test Track and Mexico pavilions is an octagonal building on platforms over a small lake called the Odyssey. The Odyssey was originally a dining location similar to Stargate or Electric Umbrella that offered standard American fare. It was unique, however, in having a Disney character musical stage show that featured Mickey Mouse and friends singing musical numbers and then coming out into the dining room to shake hands with guests in the audience.

The Odyssey closed in 1994 and would not be reused again as a regularly operational restaurant. In fact, to compensate for the loss of seats as park attendance rose again after 1994 the Electric Umbrella had the second floor dining area added during its renovation from the Stargate. The Sunshine Season Food Fair did the same in the 2005 overhaul of the Land pavilion. There seems to be no intent to reopen the area for daily operation though it is used for special events. The complex itself also houses the first aid building, child care center, and restrooms on the guest side. The backstage portion operates daily as the primary cast member cafeteria.

16. MEXICO

D URING THE OPENING of World Showcase something became immediately apparent to the general public: Mexico was the only country with a ride. To this day it remains one of only two rides and by default one of the most popular rides in the World Showcase. Other initially planned rides around the lagoon were cut to curb spending as the whole of EPCOT Center began to run beyond the planned budget. Mexico even had its ride scaled down to try and keep the costs in check.

Still, the pavilion is unique in other ways as well. While most of the World Showcase's countries focus on a layout with a plaza flanked by small themed buildings to form a square, Mexico opened with a massive show building fronted by a Mesoamerican pyramid. The pyramid structure sits directly adjacent to the World Showcase promenade and prevents the typically indecisive and meandering "flit in, flit out" approach of most guests to touring the back half of the park. In the mental game of theme park design a big decision would be forced – enter the dark and ominously looming temple or perhaps buy some tacos from the kiosk across the way.

1982-2007: The Original

Collin Campbell supervised the design of the original Mexico pavilion. On the exterior the landscaping reflects the jungle and desert regions of the country. Near the temple (which is a combination of Mesoamerican styles) there are tropical flowers placed in irregular groups to keep a wild and exotic feel for the space. The pavilion is meant to rise up from the wilds, not be a tightly controlled garden as seen in the France and the U.K. Notably the silk floss trees to the left of the temple create colorful blooms in the springtime and odd-shaped fruit. The original **Cantina de San Angel** across from the main pavilion building offers the obligatory tacos and churros with a small seating area overlooking the World Showcase lagoon.

The tiered pyramid itself rises thirty-six feet above the lagoon and leads into the 85,000-square-foot show building. The structure is flanked with stylized serpent heads to protect the sanctum of the high priest at the end of a tall flight of stairs at the top of the structure. This space is, in reality, a control booth for the fireworks show. Children are prevented from climbing the structure's steps by a carved stele of Mayan King Bird-Jaguar which pushes the first steps just up out of reach.

To the sides of the stele and stairs are the actual entrances to the pavilion which lead to a room styled as a Mayan Ceremonial Hall. This is the home of Mexico's art gallery. The first installation in the gallery was called "Splendors of the Golden Age: Three Centuries of Colonial Art." The exhibit focused on the religious fervor and the European influence that dominated Mexican art for three centuries. Artifacts such as a bullet-riddled breastplate from the 1519 Spanish conquest were displayed.

Beyond the art gallery the pavilion opens into the **Plaza de los Amigos**. The vista is supposed to be one akin to a hillside terrace of a mayoral residence in a typical Mexican town. The plaza offers an eternal nighttime setting for a bustling marketplace flanked by traditional tile-roofed buildings. Immediately inside the plaza is the bubbling **Fuente de la Vida** (the fountain of life). Various karts and kiosks run along the main floor of the interior plaza and offer souvenirs from maracas to tequila. Early sponsors of the pavilion included Cervecería Cuauhtémoc-Moctezuma and Tequila Cuervo. To the right within an alcove separate from the main plaza would have been **La Familia Fashions** which featured silver and beaded jewelry.

In the distance is another temple pyramid slightly smaller in scale the exterior. Behind the pyramid a volcano rumbles while around it a gentle river of water flows. On the plaza-side of the waterfront is the **San Angel Inn** restaurant. The San Angel is actually a Mexico City-based restaurant and the version at Epcot is operated by the same company. Toward the rear waterfront is the entrance to the boat ride and **La Princesa Cristal** – an Arribas Bros operated glass shop.

El Rio del Tiempo

The River of Time boat ride brought guests through what were considered the three cultures of Mexico: the pre-Columbian, Spanish-Colonial, and Modern Mexico. After a short switchback queue to the left of the San Angel Inn's main dining room guests would board a typical Disney-style flume ride boat. The boats would be dispatched into the lush jungle setting and round the corner to the waterfront of the San Angel Inn and the interior pyramid.

For both the boat passengers and guests of the restaurant the island-pyramid was supposed to have regular light and sound shows. The shows would have included thunder, lightning, and other effects to tell the story of how the gods wrestled the gift of music from the jealous sun and bestowed it on the earth. Hence, no sunshine in the plaza – angry jealous sun. No one encountered in researching this book remembers any of that but it is spelled out pretty clearly in early promotional literature for the park, including those produced after the park opened. Did it happen? Possibly. Was it supposed to happen but never did? Possible as well.

Beyond the scene that may-or-may-not have existed was a large stone Olmec head that marked the entrance to a cave on the boat ride path. Within the cave guests were transported through a time-tunnel back to pre-Columbian times. Old faded murals on the cave walls would become fresh and new at the end of the tunnel to depict the reversal of time. Standing squarely at the end of the tunnel was a stone sculpture of a Mayan High Priest who came to life to welcome each passing boat to his city.

The city was a mixture of ancient architecture and fairly large rear projection images. Three main scenes were presented on the screens through interpretive dance. Guests would float past these scenes quickly and likely not even see the full one-minute loop but they were fully fleshed out conceptual dances with elaborate costumes. The first was called "Nature and Science" and spoke of the ancients' understanding of man's relationship to the universe. The second, "Mathematics and Astronomy," was about the Mayan sophistication in these subjects including their understanding of the abstract concept behind the number zero. Finally, the "Quetzalcoatl and Tezcatlipoca" sequence depicted the eternal struggle between good and evil as the feathered serpent of light fought the tiger god of darkness. Other projections depicted Aztec warriors and a bustling ancient marketplace. At the end of the city sequence a screen showed the palace of Aztec king Moctezuma II who lost Mexico to Spain. The scene was exceptionally subtle, but showed Moctezuma II witnessing the fall of a comet from the sky and foretelling the downfall of his people.

Through a small transitional archway the boats would arrive in a scene called the Festival of Children which represented Mexico's colonial period. The scene was akin to something from the "it's a small world" attraction at the Magic Kingdom with its doll-like animatronics. The children sang, danced, and generally celebrated in this scene. Around the corner the boats began to enter the modern Mexico section of the ride.

A series of caves sets allowed for multiple rear-projection screens scattered around the boat path. Scenes depicted modern Mexican life through cliff diving and swim-up hotel pool bars. A particularly memorable sequence involved three large screens adjacent to the ride path that depicted merchants attempting to sell their wares by following the boats and shouting to the passengers.

For the finale the ride opened up into a large room with a night time ceiling filled with fiber optic fireworks. In the middle of the room was a large carousel full of life-size marionette-style puppets wearing traditional Mexican costumes. This scene featured the ride's theme song written by X Atencio all the way up until unload:

SINGERS: Welcome, mis amigos, to friendly Mexico. To the land of fiestas -- they're everywhere you go. Listen to marimbas and mariachis, too. Playing latin rhythms and serenading you.

2007-Present: Enter Donald

The original El Rio del Tiempo ride would close on January 2, 2007, and mark the beginning of a series of major changes to the pavilion. The general structure within the pyramid show building would remain the same but the footprint of the entire pavilion would grow to meet the demands of a growing Epcot.

Gran Fiesta Tour

El Rio del Tiempo was lagging in attendance by 2007. However, Epcot was still growing and there needed to be a stronger draw in the World Showcase to even out the crowds. The Mexican boat ride reopened as Gran Fiesta Tour starring the Three Caballeros: Donald Duck, Panchito, and Jose Carioca.

Much of the ride's internal structure and scenery remained the same. In the first scene minor modifications were made to the ride path to allow the San Angel Inn to extend further into the faux-lagoon to add twenty-five seats to its capacity. In the time tunnel instead of a Mayan there is now a screen where two of the three caballeros are looking for the missing third – Donald. Thus is the premise of the new attraction: find Donald and make it to the show in Mexico City on time.

The next scenes were not physically altered but had their projection films entirely replaced. The city scene now depicts vibrant images of modern Mexico and historic tourist sites. Amid the scenes Panchito and Jose ride around on a magical serape while Donald acts like a bumbling tourist. The pre-Columbian scene still has the little dolls throwing a party, but now they're a bit more overt with a sign declaring "Fiesta Hoy" and a few children attacking a Donald Duck piñata.

The caves sequences are many of the same scenes updated to modern footage along with cartoon overlays of Donald getting into trouble. The three screens of the overzealous merchants are replaced with a party that Panchito and Jose are physically dragging Donald away from. Finally the finale room is mostly the same but the carousel of creepy marionettes has been removed and replaced with a stage on which the Three Caballeros are in concert singing their trademark theme song.

Elsewhere around the pavilion a Donald Duck meet and greet area was added to the left of the main pyramid structure. In August of 2009 **La Cava del Tequila** replaced **La Familia Fashions** in the alcove off the main interior plaza. The new eatery and bar offers over 100 types of authentic tequila. Outside the main building old **Cantina de San Angel** closed to make way for an expanded Cantina and new **Hacienda de San Angel** restaurant. The two new locations opened September 2010 with a large building and expanded exterior dinging on the lagoon for the Cantina. The Hacienda offer casual dining for dinner with views of the nightly fireworks.

17. Norway

THE NORWAY PAVILION for years has hidden a secret in plain sight. Surrounded by the shops, trolls, and fjords is the only piece ever constructed of the long forgotten Denmark pavilion – the restrooms. This odd little remnant is a lingering reminder of the struggle to bring the World Showcase's last new international pavilion to life.

The Denmark pavilion's restrooms were first built and opened with the rest of the park in 1982 between the Mexico and China pavilions. Their non-descript structure served a functional purpose in the busy new park but as early as 1983 the plans for a Denmark pavilion had essentially fallen apart.

Instead Disney was working to convince Denmark, Norway, and Sweden to collaborate on a broader Scandinavia pavilion. For funding purposes an entity backed by a collaboration of corporations known as

ScanShow was formed. A brochure from 1983 read:

> ScanShow is planning to have the Scandinavian pavilion completed by the end of 1986, based on participation by Swedish, Danish and Norwegian companies and organizations.

Concept art was created for the pavilion and presented to various potential investors. It was to have been located between the France and United Kingdom pavilions. The design featured the architecture and culture of all three countries. By 1984 cooperation between the countries had fallen apart and appropriate funding could not be found. The Scandinavia concept became yet another failed World Showcase pavilion.

However, there were Norwegian investors still interested in a pavilion. The name of the funding entity was quickly changed to NorShow or more formally the Norwegian Showcase USA A/S. Eleven Norwegian companies and the Norwegian state together backed the pavilion. The state offered $2 million in support plus an additional $8 million in loan financing for NorShow. The total amount funded by NorShow including the Norwegian state's contributions was $33 million. The sponsorship contract was drawn up so that NorShow would share any profit from the sales of food and souvenirs with Disney. The first $3.2 million in profit would go directly to NorShow and the next $400,000 to Disney. After that, NorShow would keep sixty percent of all profits and Disney the remaining forty percent.

Funding in place, Disney sent teams of imagineers to investigate the country and create its own custom-fit pavilion. The site location within Epcot shifted back to the defunct Denmark pavilion, restrooms and all. By the spring of 1988 a group of 150 Norwegians were in place in Orlando. The shops and dining would open May 6, 1988, while the Maelstrom attraction would open with the pavilion's formal dedication on June 3, 1988.

1988-Present: High Seas Adventure

The pavilion's buildings showcase four regional styles of Norwegian architecture cobbled together: Setesdal, Bergen, Oslo and Ålesund style. Ron Bowman was the pavilion's architectural designer. Prominently displayed toward the main World Showcase promenade is the **Stave Church Gallery**. The building is a replica of the Gol Stave church found at the Norwegian Folk Museum in Oslo, Norway. The gallery inside has cycled through displays like other Epcot exhibition spaces and currently houses an exhibit on Vikings. The building is an eighty-percent scale replica of the original.

Across the main plaza is **Restaurant Akershus**, based on the castle by the same name in Oslo and serving a traditional dinner koltboard. The salt-box shaped buildings that contain the **Puffin's Roost** and **Fjording** shops are reminiscent of the Bergen and Ålesund styles. The shops feature pewter gifts by Konge Tinn, trolls by Ny-Form and ski sweaters from Dale of Norway.

Nearby the **Kringla Bakeri og Kafe** is more in the Setesdal style of architecture and offers open-faced salmon sandwiches and traditional school bread. The main attraction of the pavilion, the **Maelstrom** ride, is housed at the rear of the plaza in a continuation of the Akershus castle building.

Maelstrom

Early planning for the attraction involved the writing and art design team of Mark Rhodes and Joe Rohde who established the forthcoming Maelstrom as a passive boat ride akin to Pirates of the Caribbean and running approximately fifteen minutes in length. It would have chronicled a day in the life of a Viking from sunrise to sunset. In an early pitch meeting with Disney executives the presentation was floundering and failing to impress so Joe Rohde improvised – what if the boat suddenly went backwards after running into trolls? The executives perked up and the idea went forward.

The Maelstrom was from that point conceived as a boat ride through a troll-filled landscape of fjords and forests to be accompanied by a Sherman Bros song and culminating in a backward portion – the logistics of which were yet to be determined. It was to be wetter and rougher than the finished ride guests experience today with real rain and turbulent seas. The next presentation of the concept was to the sponsors. The Norwegian sponsors wanted a family friendly attraction and more importantly did not want the ride to focus so heavily on trolls. The sponsors wanted to see Vikings, a fishing village, polar bears, a fjord, and an oil rig. The design team, now headed by Bob Kurzweil, was left scratching their heads on how to put these ideas together into a cohesive experience. Also, the budget had been cut and the ride would need to be half the originally planned length. The time-traveling boat ride seen today is the end result.

After boarding ornate Viking-boat vehicles sculpted by imagineer Jack Ferges, guests would begin a slow climb up a lift hill into the attraction. The lift hill is flanked by stones carved with runes and hieroglyphs to give an ancient feel to the scene. A giant mask of Odin looms at the top of the hill. In Norse mythology Odin had sacrificed his eye to gain the wisdom of the ages. Beams of light radiate from Odin's single eye and as the blustering winds of a storm are heard he warns riders:

> **ODIN:** You are not the first to pass this way... nor will you be the last. Those who seek the spirit of Norway face peril and adventure, but more often find beauty and charm.

Odin closes his eye and the passenger boat coasts gently into the flume on the upper level of the building. Odin's looming voice suggests riders look first to the seafarers. Now many years back in time, guests are treated to an encampment of Vikings by the sea. This bustling area is filled with numerous animatronic figures tending to their boats. The Viking figures were fabricated by using molds left over from the World of Motion and Spaceship Earth. Soon the scene transitions to a broader view of the waterfront with ships departing into the distance. A man blows a signal horn while perched atop a rocky outcropping. It should be noted that the seeming shortness of these scenes was not the original design intent. In fact the boats travel much faster than anticipated through the flume and the animatronic programming loops for the entire attraction had to be shortened at the last minute once the discrepancy was discovered.

Next the vehicles round the corner and burst through a pair of show doors into a large scene depicting the depths of the Norwegian forest. Directly ahead an angry three-headed troll rises up – quite unhappy with the guests' presence in his forest. The massive animatronic troll was sculpted by Peter Kermode. The beast casts a spell on the boat of guests to go "back, back, over the falls" as a twinkle of fiber optics glows overhead. Much to the surprise of passengers, a unique feature of the ride mechanism then kicks in and rotates the boat to align with another flume channel. The boat is released and drops down a slope backwards into the icy polar regions of Norway's Jutenheimen mountain country. The never before seen flume ride element that allowed for this turntable effect was engineered by Dave Van Wyk.

Complete with giant polar bear figure standing on its hind paws the icy arctic is one of the most memorable scenes in the attraction. The polar bear itself was sculpted by Peter Kermode with its fur work done by Helena Hutchinson. After the polar bear encounter the boat slows to a stop with the rear end of the boat poking out of the front of the ride building's façade. Guests can look over their shoulder and out into the bustling plaza toward World Showcase, but directly ahead another troll head in a tree stump rises up and once again changes the direction of the boat.

The boat then drops forward into a turbulent storm in the North Sea near an oil rig. Pani projectors create the stormy sky above along with flashes of lightning. An early effect featuring a Tesla coil was considered to make real lightning for the scene but it was discarded when it was deemed too dangerous. The model for the oil rig was one of the few elements of the attraction not built in-house by Imagineering, but rather commissioned out to a company in Houston.

The passenger boat would then depart the storm and arrive in a small fishing village to unload. Guests would exit their vehicles and end up waiting in the nighttime plaza for the next showing of the attraction's film, **Norway-The Film,** to be ready to play. The designers of the attraction disagreed with holding guests in the area before the film, but the sponsors insisted on the idea. It had been planned originally as a pre-show experience that got switched around late in the process. Subsequently great lengths were taken by Paul Torringo and other designers to make the area interesting to wait within. *Norway-The Film* itself is only five minutes long but guests really dislike having to wait for the film and most opt-out of the experience by racing through the theater as the doors open. Norway-The Film was directed by Paul Gerber who also did the Land pavilion's *Symbiosis* and the Living Seas pavilion's *The Seas* film.

The film dramatically depicts Norway's through the eyes of a four-year-old boy. Among the featured images in *Norway-The Film* is Sognefjord, the largest of Norway's numerous fjords. There is also the Oseberg bat: a thousand-year-old Viking ship unearthed and now on display in Oslo's Viking Museum. Other imagery include a fiery nighttime view of Statoil's Statfjord B oil rig, a small fishing village on the southwest coast of Norway called Skudeneshavn, and the Holmenkollen ski resort. The film culminates in a montage of scenes of the modern (circa 1980s) Norwegian lifestyle.

During the first year of operation the Norway pavilion proved popular with over 5.7 million guests riding the Maelstrom attraction. The retail and dining locations made over $10.7 million. However, by 1992 the NorShow group backed of the pavilion entirely. They sold their stake in the pavilion back to Disney citing disappointing sales. The Norwegian government subsequently took over sponsoring the pavilion itself by contributing $200,000 a year to the pavilion until 2002. At that point the Norwegian government wanted out, and not even the embassy in Washington D.C. could convince them to stay. The pavilion has operated since without sponsorship. Helly Hensen sells its clothes in the pavilion but is not a formal sponsor. The restaurant Akershus stopped selling an authentic buffet-style Norwegian meal and was converted to a Disney Princess character-dining experience in 2005. The restaurant was renamed as Akershus Royal Banquet Hall.

As with other World Showcase films, the Norway film has become a heated issue for the Norwegian people. The film is now considered quite dated and a poor representation of modern Norway. Plans in 2003 were drawn up to redo the film, to be completed by 2005, but the project never happened. The funding for the film could not be found in Norway and it was seen as a hopelessly dead project in the Norwegian press by 2008. Without suitable Norwegian sponsorship there have been talks to redesign the pavilion back to the more general Scandinavia pavilion. In the meantime, it is now common practice to leave the doors to the theater open to allow guests to exit the ride area completely – with little regard to if the film is currently playing or not.

18. CHINA

A CCORDING TO Daoist tradition there is a mystical paradise of beauty and wonder known as the Eastern Isle of the Immortals. Depending on the mythology the location is made up of three or more mountains isolated in the Eastern Sea; primarily the islands of Fangu, Yingzhou, and Penglai. The tall and craggy peaks of the mountains create an inaccessible gateway for mere mortals and in turn offer a splendor-filled haven for immortals from the human realm. Thus sit three large craggy stones on the shore of Epcot's China pavilion.

The stones follow in the tradition of Chinese garden rock displays for the purpose of meditation. It is said the contemplation of the shape and texture of the stone would allow for the serenity of one's nature. Ancient rulers would have the best stones brought to their palace gardens through years of effort and tedious transport. Disney likely shipped the stones in as cargo on a train from a quarry in Texas, but they are at least reminiscent of one of the most prized stone types in China – the taihu. Stones culled from Lake Taihu (literally: "Grand Lake") in Jiangsu province are considered to be of particular beauty. The lake is known for producing very large stones perforated with numerous holes and indentations, much like the ones seen in Epcot, but also much like stones now found more easily and nearby in a quarry in Texas. Larger perforations in the stones at Epcot frame specially considered views of the surrounding World Showcase.

1982-2002: Wonders

The China Pavilion itself was an opening day offering of Epcot but much of what one would considered the pavilion as it is known today did not exist at the time. The entire northern complex flanking the Norway pavilion was just a simple landscaped garden. The design of the garden was meant to compliment the forthcoming Denmark pavilion – long since abandoned and later replaced with Norway's pavilion.

It is a bit disorienting to now think of the pavilion as it originally opened with only the temple complex and approach. Most guests still enter the pavilion by passing under the **Gate of the Golden Sun** and follow the water lily flanked walkway to the **Temple of Heaven** which serves as the entrance for the filmed attraction. The city of Beijing was selected as the architectural influence for the design of the entire pavilion. The aforementioned gate is formally known as a pailou, or decorated memorial archway. Old Beijing was known for having more of these archways than any other city in the world. **The Gate of the**

Golden Sun appears to be a stylized replica of the pailou at the entrance of the Yonghegong Lamasery in northern Beijing.

The circular tri-gabled building in Epcot known as the **Temple of Heaven** is actually a scale replica of a single building which along with other similar buildings made up a large complex in southern central Beijing known as the Temple of Heaven. The building represented in Epcot's China pavilion is actually the Hall of Prayer for Good Harvests. In ancient China the Emperor would go to this temple and pray for a good harvest. Being a replica, much of the symbolism of the original is preserved in the copy. The temple represents a connection between heaven and earth. Earth is represented by the shape of a square and heaven by the circle. Inside the temple the four main pillars form a square with beams connecting them upon which another circular beam rests that is connected to the twelve outer pillars. The four main pillars also symbolize the four seasons while the twelve outer pillars represent the twelve-month cycle of the Chinese calendar. The interior of the ornate building was intentionally left empty so guests could marvel at its beauty in its entirety before proceeding to the holding area of the film.

The Circle-Vision 360° film presented inside the pavilion was originally called *Wonders of China.* A unique collaboration between Disney and the Chinese government allowed for the film to be shot. Chinese crews would shoot film using the nine-camera rig in areas that outsiders/non-Chinese were not allowed to visit. This produced some spectacular shots of areas not before seen by the western audiences. The film was narrated by a fictional representation of Tang dynasty poet Li Bai (sometimes called Li Po) portrayed by actor Key Luke.

Sites seen in the film included the Great Wall, the Forbidden City, the Summer Palace, and the Qin Shi Huang Tomb. The film would unload into what was soon to be a plaza accompanied by a large shopping complex.

By the summer of 1983 the **Yong Feng Shangdian** department store was up and running at the end of the **Street of Good Fortune** which runs alongside the northern edge of the main temple complex. At 8,000 square feet the department store was considered Epcot's most ambitious shopping area at the time of construction. The success of the department store concept would lead to a shift away from smaller individual shops in Disney theme parks and to renovations like the Emporium expansion at the Magic Kingdom the next year.

Near the entrance to the attraction is a small section of the building – also accessible from the pre-show waiting area – known as the **House of the Whispering Willows** gallery. This formal art gallery is one of several located within Epcot's World Showcase and it has featured its fair share of notable expositions. An agreement was made with the Chinese government early in the life of the pavilion which allowed artifacts from the Republic of China's Palace Museum to be shown outside the country for the first time. The Palace Museum's collection was previously housed within the walls of the Forbidden City.

In April of 1984 the first fifty pieces from the museum were sent to be exhibited in Epcot including an 18th century crimson throne, jade jewelry, and other personal effects from the Qing Dynasty. These exhibitions would continue through much of the life of the pavilion and include items such as thirty antique clocks for the Artistry in Time exhibit which opened in February of 1987. Later the space would be used as a preview center for Hong

Kong Disneyland resort. The preview center took over the space in April of 2005 and was subsequently replaced by the present exhibition: Tomb Warriors: Guardian Spirits of Ancient China. The Tomb Warriors exhibit opened in 2007 and includes forty-seven pieces of ancient Chinese funerary art from the private collection of Lillian Schloss.

In July of 1984 the Denmark pavilion was officially dead as a neighbor to China and so plans moved forward to expand the China pavilion. The plan focused heavily on expanding the dining offerings of Epcot. Due to guest demand the park had already erected a temporary dining tent in the World Showcase known as the Renaissance Fair and dotted the promenade with numerous snack carts.

On September 24, 1985, the **Lotus Blossom Café** opened in the China pavilion adding 200 seats to Epcot's dining offerings. This counter service location would soon be followed on October 23, 1985, by the full-service **Nine Dragons Restaurant**. The restaurants would be situated in a new 12,000 square foot annex of the pavilion and replace the garden designed to blend with the nearby canceled Denmark pavilion. Nine Dragons added an additional 250 seats to Epcot's dining capacity. With two restaurants and a show China would become one of the most fleshed out pavilions in the entire showcase. A slightly ironic twist considering the ill-fated Denmark pavilion was in place of China in its entirety as late as 1979 in Epcot's design process.

2002-Present: Reflections

The original *Wonders of China* film closed on March 25, 2002. It was reworked with new footage to create the updated but thematically similar *Reflections of China*. The actor who portrayed Li Bai, the poet guide, in the original film had died in 1991 so a look-alike was hired for the new scenes. The narration was entirely redubbed and a new score composed by Richard Bellis. *Reflections of China* opened on May 23, 2003.

For most of its existence the shopping and dining complex in the China pavilion has been run by an operating participant known as the China Pavilion Exhibition Corporation. While the details of the exact agreement and function of the sponsorship are unknown – as the sponsorships in World Showcase are reportedly extremely competitive – it is known that the president of the company is the somewhat quirky philanthropist Dr. Nelson Ying. The physicist's family has sponsored the Epcot pavilion and every China pavilion seen at a World's Fair since 1964.

In March of 2007 a new promenade kiosk called **The Joy of Tea** opened offering hot and cold teas. More recently the Nine Dragons restaurant and Lotus Blossom Café were renovated and upgraded in 2008 to meet modern dining expectations. Early in 2011 the shopping complex of the pavilion was closed for cosmetic renovation. The interior was given more lighting and a modern look – gone are the traditional red and gold associated with the kitschy China of the past.

19. GERMANY

MYTHOLOGY takes on its own life as it spreads. It reaches new audiences who seek to interpret and explain the unknown in terms they personally comprehend. Morphing like some phantasm to appease the notions of the storyteller the facts distort and the urge to create plausibility overcomes factuality. So is the story of the Germany pavilion's fabled Rhine River Cruise attraction.

Conceptually the attraction existed, that's not up for debate, but the "what?" and "how?" are alarmingly vague from even the best sources. As the name implies, the Rhine River Cruise was to be a boat ride attraction that fully fleshed out the Germany pavilion along with a tourism display area. The tourism area is said to have been planned as a stylized town hall with medieval suits of armor and coats of arms from various German cities. A travel office at the location would have helped with arranging travel to the country itself. Whether this area was a post-show or pre-show to the attraction is unknown, but in chronological terms it was frequently mentioned in historic literature before the attraction as if it were a requisite precursor. Perhaps it was part of an amended pavilion design creating its own entry and exit plaza.

The ride itself was to have guests board a "cruise boat" for a scenic ride down the Rhine, the Tauber, the Ruhr, and the Isar rivers. The scenery of the ride would have been miniature recreations of various German landmarks that highlighted the country's past and present. Scenes were said to include the Black Forest, Oktoberfest, Heidelberg, Cologne Cathedral, and the Ruhr Valley.

The mythology of the ride commonly dictates that the entrance of the attraction was to be where the **Sommerfest** mural was painted at the rear of the pavilion adjacent to the **Biergarten** restaurant's entrance. It is said the ride's show building was completed right behind that wall with the first phase of EPCOT Center but the attraction itself was merely not installed at the time. There is some truth in this. The Rhine River Cruise had been scrapped as early as 1981. The building was constructed with it in mind, but the full extent of the ride building was not completed. Aerial photos of the pavilion reveal the show building looks like a backwards F-shape with a grassy area where much of the ride would have been. Indeed it seems the loading area was constructed and later repurposed. So what was there when the park opened?

1982-Present: Oktoberfest

The eternal Oktoberfest of the Germany pavilion with

its festive shops and old world charm was built under the consideration of the pavilion's architectural designer Ron Bowman. The building styles are derived from a variety of German styles to create a fairytale amalgamation. Following the World Showcase standard, the layout of the pavilion of has a main plaza with themed storefronts – in this case it's a German platz.

Flanking the promenade side of the platz is a row of sycamore trees which many guests will note look oddly barren in the winter months. The sort of pruning used at the pavilion is known as pollarding – a style that originated in Europe as a way to control the size of the trees in urban areas. The shop areas of the platz are decorated with numerous container gardens to add punches of controlled color. For a passably-realistic look English ivy and traditional geraniums replace more authentic German ivy-geraniums which would have wilted away in the harsh Florida climate.

As for the shops themselves, on the far left of the pavilion originally was the **Glas und Porzellan** shop featuring both Hummel and Goebel figurines. When the pavilion opened it was one of only eight locations in the entire world to carry a full collection of Hummels. In 2010 this location was renovated and turned into a popular Werther's Original Caramel shop and confectionary called **Karamell-Küche**.

Further down the left side the original line-up of stores included a shop called **Porzellanhaus** selling porcelain wares that would later be renamed **Die Weihnachts Ecke** in 1989 and focus more on Christmas items and décor. The newer shop is mostly known for its pickle-shaped tree ornaments. **Süssigkeiten** next door has mostly remained the same through the years, featuring Bahlsen brand cookies and sweets. Similarly the **Weinkeller** has seen little change and originally offered Schmitt Söhne wines. Together the left side of the pavilion created a sponsorship/participant row that would offset the costs of operating the pavilion.

The back wall of the plaza was originally only the **Biergarten** restaurant. Two additions took away some of the open space and effectively removed any vestiges of the Rhine River Cruise's intended entryway. On the left in 1989, **Kunsterbeit in Kristall** carved out a small shop area dedicated to Arribas Bros glassworks. This shop replaced a crystal kart that had sprung up in 1988 by the promenade and proved popular. On the right side **Sommerfest** was also added in 1989 offering sausages, beer, and pretzels. It added a quick-service dining location to the pavilion to feed guests who could not get reservations for the Biergarten restaurant.

Continuing clockwise around the platz would lead into **Der Teddybär** shop which remains mostly the same since the park opened with toys and dolls. Cuckoo clocks were prominently featured in the adjacent **Volkskunst**, while **Der Bücherwurm** was a creative arts bookshop. In 1999 Der Bücherwurm became **Das Kaufhaus** and began to prominently feature sportswear. The façade of the Das Kaufhaus is notable for having been modeled after the Freiburg Kaufhaus with statues of Hapsburg emperors on the second level. There are only three instead of the actual four statues on the real building to account for the reduction of scale within the pavilion.

The platz itself has a statue of St. George and the Dragon visible atop a column in the central fountain. The smell of German beer and bratwurst is constantly in the air as 26.2 miles of bratwurst are served every sixty days at the

Biergarten restaurant. Another touch of authentic old world scent comes from the nearby Old World roses planted near the promenade. These roses are varieties that were not purpose-bred over the years for brighter color and have thus retain their full fragrant aroma. The costumes of the cast members' costumes complete the effect as they reflect old Bavaria with lederhosen and dirndl skirts. So even though there is not a river cruise attraction there is some old world Germany to explore in this Epcot pavilion.

20. ITALY

How DOES the sponsor of the most popular dining location in the park end up being surprised and ousted from the World Showcase? A number of things need to occur. When the park opened **L'Originale Alfredo di Roma Ristorante** in the Italy pavilion was the most popular of the eateries around the World Showcase. The early park was more popular than planned and struggled to meet capacity needs in dining. Sponsors in other pavilions built secondary and tertiary dining locations. The company in charge of dining in the Italy pavilion, Alfredo the Original of Rome (Fla.) Inc. was tasked with adding a second 300 seat dining location across the courtyard from the original restaurant. This information was published in multiple papers as early as 1983. It never happened.

Flash forward to 2008. Alfredo's had grossed more than $20 million in the last year. The park was still struggling with meeting dining demand. **Mexico's San Angel Inc** commented to the press that the original World Showcase dining contracts were up for renegotiations and renewal. The company noted that Disney was demanding more this time around and the contracts were extremely competitive – San Angel expanded their two original locations and built another as a result of the negotiations. Twenty-five years of stagnation in the Italy pavilion and no promised second restaurant? Alfredo's was out. Insiders close to the matter say that Alfredo's management was surprised by the decision.

The Patina Restaurant Group, frequent partners with Disney at other resort destinations, was now going to operate Alfredo's location in the pavilion under a new name – and build the long promised second restaurant. So are the politics of the World Showcase.

1982-Present: L'Originale

The Italy pavilion replicates some of the most significant architectural elements of Venice. The **Doge's Palace** with its quatrefoils and elegant pattern work sits astride a scale version of the **Campanile** of St. Mark's Square. Venetian bridges, gondolas, and barber poles cement the location as distinctly Venetian. Even the promenade paving is patterned after St. Mark's Square.

Within Epcot's version of **Doge's Palace** is a shopping extravaganza of **Il Bel Cristallo** with leather handbags, jewelry, and fragrances by big name brands like Gucci, Valentino and Ferragamo. Across the plaza and beyond the sculpture of the **Lion of St. Mark** atop a column is the little shop called **Enoteca Castello**. Inside wine tasting and chocolates create thrills for the gustatory-inclined.

In the main plaza the **Theatre al Fresco** employs the traveling **World Showcase Players** group to perform audience-participatory comedic acts throughout the day.

Grapevines and olive trees further enhance the Italian theme, but the olive trees produce no fruit thanks to the high humidity of Florida. Olive oil is however quite plentiful in the pavilion and used unsparingly by the two primary restaurants. **Tutto Italia** in the old Alfredo's location at the rear left of the plaza offers traditional fare of pasta amid strolling musicians. It is joined by **Tutto Gusto**, a lighter and smaller tapas wine-bar style location that opened in the old Alfredo's pasta making area after a renovation in early 2012.

At the rear of the pavilion **Via Napoli** opened in 2010 and brought an authentic Italian pizzeria experience to the park. The wood-fired ovens within the restaurant bear the faces and names of Italy's active volcanoes: Mount Etna, Mount Vesuvius, and Stromboli.

21. UNITED STATES

SIX REVISIONS and three years of research brought the world the American Adventure. The details and honor of the World Showcase's host pavilion did not come easy. The design of the complex began with Gary Goddard and Marc Davis and then transferred to Randy Bright who became the final show writer and producer for the animatronic spectacular. The memorable theme song called "Golden Dream" was penned by Robert Moline and Randy Bright.

Originally situated at the bridge that connects Future World to World Showcase the American Adventure show would shed its modernist exterior design and find a home at the rear center of the lagoon. Additionally an originally planned third narrator, Will Rogers, would be given a smaller role in the show due to doubts from Imagineering about audiences identifying with the character. As the host pavilion the 108,000 square foot space is constructed on higher ground and surrounded by tightly controlled gardens. The features of the colonial mansion façade are specifically appointed to minimize and mask the true immense size of the pavilion. The magnolia trees, boxed hedges and annual planters are kept carefully trimmed to never betray the regal look of the entire affair.

Across from the main show building the **American Gardens Theater** offers a 900 seat venue for musical performances in an open air theater. The sycamore trees in the audience area are specifically pleached, meaning their branches are intentionally interlaced to create a living ceiling over the area. While the waterfront stage is charming, the real show lies within.

1982-Present: The American Adventure

Guests entering the pavilion enter into a large **Lower Lobby Level** with Corinthian-style columns and an ornate floor made of marble and copper. An opening in the second level allows for viewing of the oval-shaped rotunda above. The walls of the lower-lobby are covered in artwork and quotes of notable Americans such as Walt Disney, Charles A. Lindbergh, and Thomas Wolfe. An a cappella singing group known as the **Voice of Liberty** makes use of the lower level's superb acoustics to perform shows through the day.

At the appointed time guests are lead from the lower level lobby to the second floor **Holding Area** before the main show. To travel between the levels guests are brought up a series of stairs and escalators that make up the **Hall of Flags**. Forty-four historic flags of the United States hang in the gallery including the American flag in all of its forms.

The **Main Show** is held in a 1,024-seat theater complete with elegantly styled Corinthian chandeliers, columns, and paneling. The stage is flanked by the **Spirits of America**: twelve marble statues representing American qualities such as heritage, innovation, knowledge, pioneering, discovery and freedom.

The show itself is an audio-animatronic spectacular hosted by Mark Twain and Benjamin Franklin. Large set pieces seem to material from nowhere onto the stage. In reality the sets are held in a massive infrastructure akin to a sled under the raked audience seating. The stage itself has no floor and each scene rises up into place at the appointed time as the entire sled structure holding the scenes silently advances. The show itself has undergone minor updates over the years, particularly to the finale projection montage, but it has always included great Americans such as Frederick Douglass, Susan B. Anthony, Alexander Graham Bell, John F. Kennedy, and Martin Luther King Jr.

Details like the integration of Will Rogers own quotes into his depression era speech bring a unique authenticity to the production. The song "Brother Can You Spare a Dime?" was heavily researched to be historically accurate as possible. Franklin D. Roosevelt's unusual presidential seal was carefully copied for his podium in the show. Great care was put into each scene to make sure the characters truly felt alive, from the gentle rocking of Benjamin Franklin in his chair to the shivering of Washington's soldiers in the winter snow.

The show culminates in the song "Golden Dreams" along with a project montage which has allowed through the years for minor updates to the finale of the show. At the end of the show guests are returned to the showcase promenade to explore the adjacent **Liberty Inn** counter-service restaurant. In 2004 the lobby area of the attraction had a gallery space added known as the **American Heritage Gallery**. It showcases a series of authentic American artifacts on loan from various collections such as the Walt Disney-Tishman Collection, the Henry Ford Museum, and the Mark Twain House and Museum.

22. JAPAN

CRITICS WERE not fond of the Japan pavilion when it first opened with the park in 1982. In reviews it was given one out of three stars, three out of ten stars, and called "pretty but boring." In particular the critics were unhappy with the lack of an attraction in the Japan pavilion. Besides dining, the early critics couldn't fathom any reason to linger in the area.

Perhaps the critics were subconsciously keying into the intended design of the pavilion. The **Meet the World** show had been axed late in the development of the pavilion but not heavily advertised the way the forthcoming **Horizons** ride or even the abandoned **South Africa** pavilion were. There is an inherent sense of flow toward the back of the Japan pavilion where it abruptly dead ends. Back in that area is where the show entrance was supposed to be.

And just what was this show? It was a rotating theater

experience with multiple-scenes akin to the **Carousel of Progress** called **Meet the World**. It was meant to introduce guests to the cultural heritage of Japan as they "*meet the world with love.*" The show featured an animated crane explaining Japanese history to a young boy and girl. Development of the attraction concept was spurred by Konosuke Matsushita, founder of the Matsushita Electric Industrial Company. He had a strong interest in Japanese history as well as Walt Disney's philosophy and pressed Disney to create a Japanese attraction comparable to the **Hall of Presidents** or **Carousel of Progress** attractions. For reasons unknown, **Meet the World** opened instead in **Tokyo Disneyland** which opened in 1983. It was sponsored there by the Matsushita Electric Industrial Company.

Meet the World wouldn't be the last concept for the pavilion to be shelved. As the years went by multiple attractions were considered from a bullet-train simulation to a Matterhorn-style roller coaster through Mt. Fuji. None, it would seem, could find financial backing from Japan or urgency for completion within the Disney company.

1982-Present: Meticulous Oasis

Gary Goddard guided the design of the Japan pavilion working along with Claude Coats and Herb Ryman. The empty attraction building in the rear has a façade meant to be a replica of the **Shirasagi-Jo**, a 17th century fortress overlooking the Japanese city of Himeji. Hidden in a back corner of the gateway into the fortress is the **Bijutsu-Kan** gallery. This art gallery has hosted exhibits on Japanese culture ranging from the art of kites to an exhibition on ancient mythical spirits as portrayed in popular media.

Leading up to the fortress and taking up most of the pavilion's space is the **Mitsukoshi Department Store** and its second-floor restaurants. The Mitsukoshi complex is contained within the **Shishinden**, inspired by the ceremonial and coronation hall found in the Imperial Palace grounds at Kyoto. The main department store on the lower level is an extension of the Mitsukoshi brand, established in 1673 and one of the oldest and largest department store chains in existence. Within its large footprint guests find numerous wares from ceramics and tableware to magna and anime – there is even a sake tasting bar and a Mikimoto pearl shop.

The restaurants above the store have undergone some cosmetic changes through the years. The **Teppanyaki Dining Room, Tempura Kiku**, and the **Matsu No Ma Lounge** opened with the pavilion. The **Teppanyaki Dining Room** offered chef prepared stir-fried foods on a hot grill table in front of guests, the other two locations offered tempura (fried food) and sushi. In 2007 the restaurants underwent renovations to modernize and update their interiors. The **Teppanyaki Dining Room** became **Teppan Edo** but still offers the same general cuisine. **Tempura Kiku** and the **Matsu No Ma Lounge** became a single restaurant called **Tokyo Dining** that offers a selection of traditional Japanese cuisine.

Across from the Mitsukoshi complex is the hilltop **Yakitori House**, a small version of the **Shoken-tei** in the **Kyoto Imperial Villa** gardens. The **Yakitori House** functions as the pavilion's quick-service dining location. It features an outdoor seating area with hanging lanterns and a small stream that cascades over the hillside and down into a traditional **Koi Pond**. The gardens of the pavilion are tightly controlled in the traditional Japanese style. Many of the plants are native to Japan: nearly ninety percent. Other countries of World Showcase almost exclusively have look-alike plantings but Japanese plants are able to thrive in the Florida climate. To stay within the Japanese style, plantings within the pavilion are grouped in numbers of three, five, or seven items for symbolic purposes. Sound is also important so a traditional bamboo clacker chimes out near the **Yakitori House** at the head of the stream.

Near the **Koi Pond** at the base of the hill is the blue-roofed, five-story **Goju-no-to Pagoda**, inspired by a shrine built at Nara in 700 A.D. The stunning building is topped with a bronze nine-ringed sorin with gold wind chimes and a water flame. At its base **Taiko Drummers** perform daily shows. Other entertainment in the pavilion originally included candy art, ikebana, sumi-e, and origami demos. Only the candy art remains today, with the artist forming miniature sculptures from pieces of warm gum candy.

Finally, across the promenade and set out into the World Showcase lagoon is the **Tori Gate**. The gate is styled after the one found at Itsukushima and functions as a welcoming symbol to the entire world beyond.

23. MOROCCO

WORLD SHOWCASE was meant to expand from the original opening day offerings. Following that mentality the Morocco pavilion was added to the showcase in September of 1984 – the first new pavilion since the park opened. At the time it was seen as a first step in filling out the back of the park with various nations. In reality, it would be one of only two additions made in World Showcase since the park opened. Early news accounts even reported the plans to have five new pavilions installed before the end of the first three years. Morocco was the only one of those plans to see the light of day.

1984-Present: Pride and Prayer

A detailed replica of a famous prayer tower, the **Koutoubia Minaret**, stands guard over the entrance to the

Morocco pavilion. Three cities are presented architecturally by the pavilion: Casablanca, Fez, and Marrakesh. In the center of the rectangular courtyard is a replica of the **Najjarine Fountain** lined with thousands of multi-colored tiles. The showcase is styled like most Moroccan cities and divided into two sections representing the new and old: the **Ville Nouvelle** and the **Medina**.

In the **Medina** portion of the pavilion the attention to detail can simply be called stunning. King Hassan II of Morocco sent his own artisans to carve, tile, and detail the buildings as only a native could. In fact, at the time of opening the Morocco pavilion was the only country in the World Showcase sponsored by the country and not a corporation. The maze of shops is filled with magical offerings and a few surprises for curious minds. The shops sell a sampling of the handicrafts for which Morocco is famous such as handcrafted straw bags, traditional beaded headdresses, finger cymbals, and elegant carpets. The sunlight beams through the false timbers of the open air plaza's roof – kept dry by a hidden glass ceiling during the frequent Florida downpours.

Cultural representatives from Morocco who come to Epcot to represent their country are warned of the Florida climate in advance. They are told that while it is hot in Morocco it's the humidity that will exhaust them in Florida. For further cultural authenticity Moroccan art is featured around the pavilion and guests may inquire about the 45-minute guided **Treasures of Morocco Tour** that is offered throughout the day.

Directly to the left at the entrance of the pavilion is the often-overlooked **Gallery of Arts and History**. Like other Epcot exhibition spaces this small museum has offered a series of authentic collections on display over the years.

The current exhibition is **The Moroccan Style: The Art of Personal Adornment** featuring ornate jewelry and clothing from the country. To the right of the gallery is the **Fez House**. The house is presented as an authentic representation of a traditional Moroccan home with beautiful mosaic tiles, carvings, and artifacts such a weaving loom.

In the rear of the pavilion the **Marrakesh Restaurant** offers full-service dining with African flare. Cinnamon spiced beef and melon create an exotic experience for the American palate. The interior is styled as a Moroccan fortress and features floor shows of belly dancers. Back in the plaza the counter-service **Tangierine Café** serves a variety of Moroccan sandwiches and specialty pastries like baklava.

Speaking of food, the pavilion is landscaped with a heavy emphasis on the agriculture of Morocco, one of the country's leading industries. Sour orange trees, mint, ornamental cabbages, olive trees, and date palms can be found spread throughout the pavilion.

Across the promenade near the **Friendship Dock** on the lagoon side is the **Berber Oasis**. The tent offers handicrafts and henna tattoo service. Next door a small stage is set up for the pavilion's most popular entertainment offering, **MoRockin**, an Arabic rock band with belly dancer accompaniment.

24. FRANCE

THE EIFFEL TOWER replica in the France pavilion is 103 feet tall. Considering the real thing is 1,063 feet tall, you can do some relative scaling and say the France pavilion in World Showcase is one-tenth the Paris but all of the charm. The pavilion reflects the ambiance of France between 1870 and 1910, a period known as La Belle Époque, or "the beautiful time." It was a period of plentiful art, literature, grand exhibitions, inventions, and science; a time when the distinctive style and character of France as the world knows it came to be.

1982-Present: La Belle Époque

France has always been one of the most popular locations in the World Showcase. Shortly after opening plans were put into action to expand the dining options to meet guest demand. The sidewalk café of **Au Petit Café** was closed and became the glass covered dining section of the expanded **Chefs de France** restaurant. The more formal **Bistro de Paris** opened on the second floor of the restaurant complex by June of 1984 offering even more selection, and finally the **Boulangerie et Patisserie** had to move down the path to a larger location to serve the hordes. The restaurants, all of them, are run by The France Chefs – Paul Bocuse, Gaston Lenotre, Roger Verge, and associate Didier Fouret. Thanks to this association Epcot has played host to the world renowned Bocuse d'Or culinary competition.

Just beyond the restaurant complex is **La Promenade**, or avenue, styled as a typical Parisian path would be; lined with tree ascending the incline. In Paris these would be linden trees, but in Florida's harsh tropical climate the effect is created with Natchez crape myrtle. Nearby is the embroidered parterre **Le Notre Garden** where 985 shrubs are shaped into the fleur-de-lis design. Crape myrtle trees also substitute for the lilacs found in France and provide significant color as they bloom in the spring.

Along the way guests can stop into the Guerlain boutique of **La Signature** shop. There they can purchase one-of-a-kind perfumes, make-up and personal accessories at one of only two such shops in the world. The novel concept allows for a professional beauty consultation within a theme park. Across the arcade is the **Plume et Palette** full of fine French fragrance lines. When the pavilion first opened **Plume et Palette**, as its name suggests, was actually a bookstore. An iron stairway would lead to a second floor gallery filled with portfolios of art prints for purchase – much like the many smaller art museums found throughout Paris. The works of Monet,

Renoir, and Toulouse-Lautrec could be thumbed through in the early days of the pavilion.

On the offshoot path known as **La Petite Rue,** the **L'Esprit de la Provence** shop provides a taste of southern France through dinnerware, tableware, and decorative items including those of Barton & Guestier and Guye Larouche. It is a wonderful place to pick of a ceramic salt pig or a bar of lavender scented soap. The attached **Les Vins de France**, sponsored by George DuBoeuf, offers wine tasting and an admirable champagne selection. At the end of **La Promenade** is the signature attraction of the pavilion – and importantly, the last opening day attraction remaining in Epcot.

Impressions de France

The **Palais du Cinéma** presents the film *Impressions de France*. The film is shown on five screens providing a 200-degree panorama. Film as an art form is a distinctly French philosophy. While Americans may enjoy film, the French revel in it. Movie houses showing older art films are dotted throughout Paris. It is in this vein that Impressions de France has lasted without any significant updates since the park opened in 1982. Spectacular views offered by the film include Versailles, the towers of Mont St. Michel, fabled French chateaus, Mont Blanc, La Rochelle, Cannes, the Arc de Triomphe, and the ski slopes of the Alpine mountainsides.

The stunning film was co-produced by Rick Harper and Bob Rogers of WDI. The narration is voiced by Claud Gobet. The musical score includes pieces from Claude Debussy, Camille Saint Saens, and Francois-Adrien Boieldieu performed by the London Symphony Orchestra.

The scenes themselves are meant to play out like a moving landscape painted by Monet, Utrillo or Degas.

After the film guests are deposited into an iron and glass covered shopping plaza reminiscent of Paris' now-demolished **Les Halles** shopping district. An intended addition to this area was to be an interactive map of France. By pushing a button guests would learn about what was going on in the various regions of France. This feature never came to exist despite appearing in early literature after the grand opening of the park.

Early concepts for the French pavilion included Place du Tertre – an artist colony – and the cathedral of Sacré Cœur. Neither looked unequivocally French the way the mansard roofs and the **Eiffel Tower** of the final pavilion do. Also considered were the Moulin Rouge and Place Pigalle though the French advisors considered the latter tacky.

25. United Kingdom

EARLY LITERATURE for the United Kingdom pavilion reminisced on "a nation of shopkeepers." It was an odd choice of phrase for Disney to use in explaining how the United Kingdom pavilion represented the British people in 1982. Certainly the U.K. pavilion is still shops, shops, and more shops – not to mention a restaurant/pub – but perhaps reiterating an insult previously used by Napoleon I as to why Britain would not be able to withstand his forces was a lapse in judgment. However, the shops of the U.K. pavilion are a unique entity in the World Showcase.

1982-Present: Keep Shopping

Straddling the main promenade, the U.K. pavilion must be walked through in order to pass. Other pavilions may have a kiosk or two on the waterfront but the U.K. has the promenade meander directly through its façades. The overall design is a compression of styles from around the nation into a single block reflecting a cluster of periods. Buildings range in styles including: London Victorian, Yorkshire Manor, Tudor, Georgian, Hyde-Park, Regency, and a Shakespearean cottage. There are even two different castles depicted: King Henry's Court and Sir Walter Scott's. The cast members wear Tudor style costumes.

The primary feature of the pavilion is the **Rose & Crown Pub and Dining Room**, presented by Bass Exports Ltd. The building is typical Victorian English with its etched glass panels, dark mahogany bar and authentic dart board. The pub's crown bullion window panes were cut from hand-blown glass discs that came directly from Britain. Nearby the **Yorkshire County Fish and Chips** shop does brisk business on the waterfront – sales from the location account for nearly 50% of the food sales at the pavilion. The fish and chips shop was previously sponsored by Harry Ramsden from 1999 until 2004.

There is a perennial garden on the southern side of the pavilion that is filled with flowers that attract butterflies. The butterfly garden has a chrysalis box where thirty-five butterfly chrysalises are pinned for display each week. Nearby a **Knot Garden** flanks the replica of Anne Hathaway's 1500s-style thatched-roof cottage containing the **Tea Caddy** shop. The garden grows a variety of herbs year-round. It leads into a **Hedge Maze** with walls of Japanese yew styled like the Somerleyton Hall Maze built in 1846 in England. Nearby is a **Bandstand** which features a Beatles cover band throughout the day.

The **Tea Caddy** shop itself operates in collaboration with Twinings Tea and sells many of their products along with English cookies and other goodies like Cadbury chocolates. Next door and connected to the **Tea Caddy** is the **Queen's Table** which specializes in Royal Doulton Fine China and high end fragrances. The crests of four major schools (Oxford, Cambridge, Eton, and Edinburgh) can be seen in the upstairs window of the **Queen's Table**.

An operating participant, the Historical Research Center, Inc., staffs the **Heraldry Shop** allowing guests to look up their family heritage and crest. The **Sportsman Shoppe** was previously sponsored by the Pringle of Scotland and offered sweaters, knits, kilts, and tartans. The **Toy Soldier** features games, stuffed animals, toys and books from English Disney characters such as Winnie the Pooh, Alice in Wonderland and Peter Pan.

Imagineers spent three years researching the United Kingdom pavilion. The original design called for a large train station styled like Kings Cross station toward the rear of the pavilion just beyond where the bandstand can now be found. Originally it was to be home to a tour of the country (possibly something akin to Japan's once planned train simulation) but eventually it became thought of as a space for a Victorian music and dining hall. The English conception of a music hall, however, is far bawdier and risqué than Disney was willing to put in their theme park and the idea was subsequently discarded.

Small touches do make for a major impact in this relatively inauspicious pavilion though. Traditional **Red Telephone Booths** set the mood for a distinctly British experience for most Americans. They may be called:

Right Booth: 407.827.9861
Left Booth: 407.827.9862
Center Booth: 407.827.9863

26. CANADA

LUMBERJACKS. There were to be no lumberjacks in the Canada pavilion. The country did not want to be portrayed in that light. While there are no actual lumberjacks nearly all of the cast members working within the pavilion wear red flannel shirts as part of their costume. It is as if Disney was determined to make a statement about Canada and lumberjacks. It doesn't help that the original pavilion design – the one that was actually partially constructed – included numerous giant fake pine trees to give it a deep woodsy feel. They even got as far as having numerous giant tree stalks installed before someone in Disney vetoed the idea. The branch-free stalks were then sadly removed. Perhaps they hired some real lumberjacks to chop them down.

Those trees were reportedly removed due to looking out of scale from around the World Showcase lagoon, but one can't help but imagine an angry Canadian sponsor shouting: "We're not lumberjacks!"

1982-2007: The Original

While there are not any lumberjacks or giant pine tree forests - the pavilion as it came to exist does include the largest and most labor-intensive garden in the showcase. The meticulously maintained grounds of the faux **Victoria Butchart Gardens** feature a wide selection of ever-changing seasonal blooms.

The Canada pavilion in World Showcase at Epcot also includes examples of buildings and scenes found across the nation. A romantic hotel is replicated in the **Hotel du Canada** which houses a gift boutique. A nearby waterfront area is designed to reflect the look of the Eastern seaboard, while the **Victoria's Butchart Gardens** were patterned to represent a West-coast style. The display proudly includes blooms such as snapdragons, begonias, impatiens, geraniums and viola.

The **Hotel du Canada** itself is a distinctive 19th century French chateau-style building, modeled after Ottawa's chateau Laurier. It boasts a scenic view of the faux-**Rocky Mountains** with waterfalls and abandoned mines as a backdrop. When the park opened the restaurant in the basement of the **Hotel du Canada** was merely a buffeteria to serve the masses. **Le Cellier** later became a fine dining location and as of 2012 is considered one of the high-end dining locations on property. It's a very impressive a climb for what began as such an unassuming little restaurant.

Around the front of the building is the main entryway to the pavilion with a series of steps up the front face of the **Rocky Mountains** and **Hotel du Canada**. At the first landing is what's meant to be a **Native Indian Village**. The area is marked with 30-foot totem poles and a log cabin. Only one of the totem poles is real wood, the other two are fiberglass. The real totem pole was carved by British Columbian artist David Boxley and added to the pavilion in 1998. The totem depicts the raven tricking the sky chief into releasing the sun, moon, and stars into the universe from a chest.

The nearby **Northwest Mercantile** trading post carries authentic Canadian crafts, boutique items, and a Roots clothing store. In 1996 an agreement between Disney and the Royal Canadian Mounted Police allowed Disney to sell the first-ever authentic Mounties-branded merchandise. There is also plush of Disney characters dressed as lumberjacks.

Further up the face of the pavilion, a plaza provides a scenic overlook. The **Rocky Mountain** area that makes up the rear of the pavilion has thirty foot cascading waterfalls creating great photo opportunities for guests. A small store on the side of the path called **La Boutique des Provinces** was open in the upper level of the **Hotel du Canada** building from September 1986 until January 2005. The shop featured fine china and Anne of Green Gables merchandise. The closure of the shop location apparently was because of waning attendance to the pavilion's show. Even in the early days of the pavilion an elevator shaft was installed between the shop and the restaurant below per the original design specifications. However, the elevator mechanism itself was never installed as the World Showcase under construction ran out of funding. The shaft would be boarded up on both ends and eventually become **Le Cellier's** original wine cellar.

A steep climb down a series of steps guides guests down amid the waterfalls and into the cave-like entrance of the *O Canada* film's theater in the **Maple Leaf Mine.** The mine's name itself was hastily changed after the grand opening of the pavilion.

The story goes: The LaBatt Brewing Company was one of the original sponsors of the Canada pavilion and had representatives on site for the grand opening celebration. They insisted Disney change the name of an abandoned mineshaft entrance to the attraction upon seeing it. It had been originally been titled **Moosehead Mine** – the name of LaBatt's direct competitor.

O Canada

The film in the Canada pavilion opened with the park as fairly standard Circlevision 360° film with sweeping scenic vistas of the country. Notable scenes included the Bluenose fishing schooner, pine-covered mountains at Banff National Park, reindeer in the Northwest Territories, and the northern midnight sun.

The film was always a bit dry, and even the theme song was of questionable authenticity. The lyrics included both English and French verses – verses which many French Canadians would claim were butchered by the singer beyond any acceptable level of conversational French. By 1987 Canada itself wanted the pavilion to be updated. Plans were set into motion to provide $1 million in funding for a new film. At the time the Canadian tourism ministry official Michael Forrestall boasted that only Canada and Morocco actively supported their own pavilions in the showcase. For reasons unknown the 1987 update of the pavilion fell through.

2007-Present: Martin Short

By 2007 the Canadian Tourism Commission reported to the press that they were getting numerous complaints from Canadians who visited the pavilion. They felt it did not represent modern Canada and that the country was more than geese, lumberjacks, and flannel jackets. The CTC pointed out that the scenes for the original film were originally shot in 1979 and were now vastly outdated. Something needed to be done.

In September of 2007 an updated version of the film opened with Canadian comedian and actor Martin Short as the host and narrator. The old song and lack of an authentic French-Canadian voice was also addressed as Eva Avilia, the 2006 Canadian Idol winner, was selected to sing the theme song "Canada, You're a Lifetime Journey." The new film repurposed some of the old film but is generally up to date. It takes guests from New Brunswick's Bay of Fundy to the western beauty of British Columbia and the 800-year-old redwood trees of Cathedral Grove. The film is generally considered a success. At the same time, it's still not bringing enough foot traffic to the highest tier of the pavilion to warrant the reopening of the shuttered **La Boutique des Provinces** shop.

27. WORLD SHOWCASE MISC

THERE ARE A FEW tidbits worth mentioning about the World Showcase area of the park that do not fit cleanly into the discussion of the various pavilions.

World Showplace

During the **Millennium Celebration** a large tent was erected in the World Showcase between the Canada and United Kingdom pavilions known now as the **World Showplace Special Events Center**. Originally it was called the **Millennium Village** and featured mini-pavilions of multiple countries for the duration of the celebration. Think of it as **Innoventions** for countries.

Brazil had a section dedicated to the rainforest. **Chile** had guests harvesting drinking water from clouds. The **Eritrea** display had guests partaking of a coffee ceremony.

Israel offered a simulator ride through Jerusalem. **Saudi Arabia** had a virtual reality tour of the country. **Scotland** let guests play miniature golf. Finally, **Sweden** had twenty-seven foot eggs that talked about Swedish innovations. There was also a section for **Expo 2000**, the World's Fair of 2000 in Hanover, Germany. It showed how the eight nations represented helped each other improve the quality of life for their population. **Ethiopia, Indonesia, Israel, Kenya, Namibia, New Zealand, India** and **South Africa** were represented through **Expo 2000**. Artisans from **Lebanon, Peru, Thailand, Egypt, Greece, Korea** and **Venezuela** also did presentations of their skills.

When the fifteen month celebration was over the space became the special events pavilion. It occupies what could be an expansion area for a whole new country pavilion in the World Showcase as well as the rear side of the United Kingdom pavilion's plot.

The Outpost

Between China and Germany is a tiny location that is mildly African themed known as the Outpost. A full-fledged **Equatorial Africa** pavilion was planned for the location and even advertised as coming soon as the park opened. It never actually materialized. The pavilion is long forgotten and likely to never be built as other aspects of Africa are now represented in the Animal Kingdom theme park. The **Refreshment Outpost** snack bar opened in June of 1983 and was later sponsored by Coca Cola. The plot of land being blocked by this tiny drink cart is the largest available open space around the entire World Showcase. It is massive in size and capable of holding two complete pavilions or one very large country pavilion. For a time the

Russia pavilion was going to be constructed in this space, but those plans also fell apart.

Fireworks Spectaculars

On October 23, 1982, the first fireworks and laser show on the **World Showcase Lagoon** called *Carnival de Lumiere* opened. It was a small show that used rear projection screens that could only be viewed from the promenade between the Mexico and Canada pavilions. In the summer of 1983 an updated show named *A New World Fantasy* debuted. It utilized the same screens and much of the same technology as *Carnival de Lumiere*.

On June 9, 1984, the next show, *Laserphonic Fantasy*, opened. It was a larger production that could be viewed from multiple angles around the lagoon. It relied on mist screens for the laser projections. It featured the first use of non-continuous lines in a laser animation and was the first use of laser graphics on a water-droplet screen.

On January 30, 1988, the first version of *Illuminations* opened. It featured many repurposed elements of the earlier shows but mixed them with a full orchestral score instead of the previous synthesizer music.

For the twenty-fifth anniversary of Walt Disney World a new show called *IllumiNations 25* was produced and opened on September 21, 1996. The show lasted only a year and was replaced by a second version also called *IllumiNations 25*. It remained a tribute to Walt Disney World, but much of the classical music returned to the show. The twenty-fifth anniversary elements of the show were subsequently stripped from the show in February of 1998 and it continued to play under the name *IllumiNations*.

Finally a whole new show called *Illuminations 2000: Reflections of Earth* opened on September 23, 1999. The new show introduced many new elements such as the inferno barge, earth globe, perimeter firework rounds, and the large propane torches around the perimeter of the lagoon. It was designed as part of the **Millennium Celebration** and tied into the overall presentation.

Unbuilt Pavilions

When the park opened it was announced that five new World Showcase pavilions would be built within the first three years of operations. During that period only Morocco was built. **Spain, Israel, Denmark, Equatorial Africa, Russia** and **Switzerland** have all seriously been considered at some point.

The countries of **India** (1986), **Turkey** (1988), and **South Korea** (2002) have approached Disney about being included in the showcase but were turned away. **Turkey** was told they just weren't looking for another pavilion at the time and **South Korea** was told it just wouldn't bring in enough visitors to justify the expense of building the pavilion.

CPSIA information can be obtained at www.ICGtesting.com
Printed in the USA
BVOW041852051212

307410BV00006B/181/P

9 781456 589660